Identity Theft

Finding the missing person in you

John Andrews

New Wine Press

New Wine Ministries
PO Box 17
Chichester
West Sussex
United Kingdom
PO19 2AW

ISBN 978-1-905991-11-2

Typeset by CRB Associates, Reepham, Norfolk
Cover design by CCD, www.ccdgroup.co.uk
Printed in Malta

Dedication

Alex and Ruth Andrews
My pop and wee mo'er

God is His infinite mercy saw fit to place me into the care
of the greatest parents any person could ever have.
My life is rich and blessed because of your lavish love,
generous investment, unflinching support and
continuous encouragement.

I love you so very, very, very much.
Thank you for everything.

"Every good and perfect gift is from above,
coming down from the Father of heavenly lights . . . "
(James 1:17)

Contents

Acknowledgements

A massive contribution has been made by so many people in helping to bring this book to birth. I am one of many.

To Dawn, my bestest friend in the whole wide world. Thank you for your patience, encouragement and generosity. You're delicious and I love you.

To Elaina, Simeon and Beth-Anne – possibly my greatest fans (and a constant source of illustrations!) Ta muchly.

To my wonderful proofers, Dawn Andrews, Pippa Ankers, Marion Hancock and Marina Watts, you're brill! I'm so grateful for your generous support and patient endurance in trying to straighten out my grammar.

To Stuart Bell for writing the foreword for this book.

To Tim and all at New Wine Press for believing in this book and helping to make it happen.

Finally, to my heavenly Father. Even when I wasn't sure who I was, You never had any doubts. I'm living more like a son because You have never given up on me, persisting to shed light on the path of my pilgrimage. Your grace has permitted me to catch a glimpse of Your abundant Father-heart and the privilege of my sonship. With all that I am, I thank You.

Hustled Out of Inheritance

A leaflet came through my door recently. It informed me, "Your identity and personal information are valuable". It urged me to protect my identity and personal details as vigorously as possible from those who would exploit such facts for their own criminal ends.[1] Since the year 2000, crimes against our identity have skyrocketed. In the UK alone, thousands of people have had their identities compromised or stolen, costing the government and the economy, not to mention the individuals in question, billions of pounds and a whole heap of misery. In the most extreme cases where a person's identity has been thoroughly compromised, some victims have had to declare themselves *legally dead* to resolve the situation, a phenomenon known as "psuedocide"!

Though it is a relatively new crime for our society, the first recorded act of identity theft took place thousands of years ago. It involved an unsuspecting couple who had the world at their feet and a criminal mastermind, the director of an agency skilled in the art of deceit and theft. Their encounter and the subsequent consequences give us insight into the importance of our personal identity and the priority that we must give to understanding and protecting it. The stated aim of this criminal agency, which incredibly still exists today, is to "... steal, kill and destroy", to

attack our identities so mercilessly that we are left at best confused
and at worst destroyed. This is a day like no other when we need
to protect our identity because our very lives depend on it.

The magnificence of the setting in which this crime took place
was in stark contrast to the brutality of the encounter itself. Its
name was Eden. In Hebrew that means *delight*, and it certainly
lived up to its name. Its beauty was breathtaking, the larder was
full with abundant provision, and those living there, human and
animal alike, experienced only peace and harmony. A river flowed
out of this place dividing into four streams. The Pishon went
around the land of Havilah where gold was found; the Gihon
flowed around the whole land of Cush; the Tigris flowed in front
of Assyria and the Euphrates. To top it off, Adam and Eve, the
only human inhabitants of Eden at this stage, owned it all! The
generous benefactor who had planted and established the garden,
handed the title deeds over to His friends with only one restrictive
clause:

> *"You are free to eat from any tree in the garden; but you must not eat
> from the tree of the knowledge of good and evil, for when you eat it you
> will surely die."*
>
> (Genesis 2:16–17)

Sounds like a pretty good deal to me. Unfortunately, such beauty
and wealth attracted the attention of the criminal fraternity and it
wasn't long before they were trying to muscle their way in, in
order to hustle the current inhabitants out. Somehow they
discovered the details of the clause which became the vehicle of
the hustle.

> *"For God knows that when you eat of it* [the forbidden tree] *your eyes
> will be opened, and you will be like God, knowing good and evil."*
>
> (Genesis 3:5)

The dictionary defines "hustle" as "to shake, to toss frequently, to shake to and fro". In modern usage the ideas is to so disorientate a victim that they make bad choices based on wrong assumptions.

Have you ever been hustled?

I thought I had him. Proud of my bargaining skills and an unexpected level of courage, I apparently talked the salesman of African curios down to half the price we started at. He complained a lot, spoke of his children needing an education and generally how hard his life was ... all the while making me feel like it was my fault. My resolve faltered and I voluntarily raised the price, not by much, but by enough to generate an expansive tooth-filled smile and an immediate deal. I had helped that "poor man" and still managed to get a "great" deal. Later that week I visited the craft centre where most of the items I had bought were made. I managed to get into the wholesale area, where these crafts were sold to traders, like my poor friend. When I saw the prices they were being sold for and what I had paid, I realised I had been well and truly hustled and that my "poor African friend", was laughing all the way to the bank. God bless him!

The subtle brilliance of the approach made to Eve is that it combined a truth and a lie in one sentence. The bait of the truth disguised the hook of the lie.

The truth was: *"For God knows that when you eat of it your eyes will be opened, knowing good from evil."*

The lie was: *"... and you will be like God ... "*

But why was this a lie? **Because Adam and Eve were already like God!**

No, not in the absolute, Almighty Creator and Sustainer of the universe sense, but as human beings they were the perfect representation of their Creator God.

> *"So God created man*
> *in his own image,*

> *in the image of God*
>   *he created him;*
> *male and female*
>   *he created them."*

(Genesis 1:27)

If they were not sure of who they were, then they could be convinced that they needed to be someone else or something more. However, in a very real sense, they could not be any more like God than they already were. This was the deadly hook at the heart of the bait.

This story is not about a piece of fruit from a tree . . . it is about identity, authority and destiny.

The devil (the criminal mastermind in question), understood the dynamic link between the three things. He knew that if Adam and Eve became confused about who they were, it would undermine their authority to lead and execute the plans of God, which would, in turn, threaten to destroy their destiny in God. The devil understands, more than most followers of Jesus, that our God-given identity produces divine authority to fulfil our ultimate destiny.

Adam and Eve ate of the fruit and the rest, as they say, is history. However, the immediate impact on that first human community teaches us lessons that we would do well to observe and learn from. The chaos which ensued was not just because they ate the fruit, but because they didn't truly know who they were.

Influential authority

> *"She also gave some to her husband, who was with her, and he ate it."*
(Genesis 3:6)

Eve naturally shared her new found experience with her husband and influenced him to eat. In the New Testament Paul suggests strongly that Adam was not deceived by the serpent, but rather he ate of the fruit because of Eve who was the one misled.[2] From her experience and journey, she led him to the same path. It seems clear that his main reason for eating was because of her.

Whether we try to or not, we influence other people, especially those close to us. They are impacted positively or negatively by our beliefs, conclusions and behaviour. If we are secure in our identity, living strong and attractive lives, then those around us will be touched by that fruit. Conversely, if we live out of insecurity of identity and confusion about the truth, this will impact the people we touch and they will be influenced to eat of the same fruit we're eating from.

It is important to know who you are, because you are going to influence somebody. That somebody may be your spouse, a family member, a work colleague, a follower or a complete stranger, but like it or not, you and the fruit you are feeding yourself on touches somebody every day. You may want to deny such a thing is happening, but I suggest to you, it is virtually impossible not to influence people, unless we decide to cut ourselves off from them entirely and even then we'll influence them by our absence!

Eve's influential authority encouraged Adam to eat. Who are you influencing and with which *who* are you influencing them?

Personal vulnerability

> "... they realised that they were naked ... "

> (Genesis 3:7)

In *The Mask Behind the Mask*, the biographer Peter Evans says that actor Peter Sellers played so many roles he sometimes was not sure of his own identity. Approached once by a fan who asked him, "Are you Peter Sellers?" Sellers answered briskly, "Not today!" and walked on.[3]

God made Adam and Eve naked because that was the way He designed them to be. Their nakedness reflected their purity, innocence, openness, acceptance and transparency. As children of God, in the delight of Eden, secure in who they were, there was no need to cover up or be ashamed. Their sense of identity produced complete freedom. But once "their eyes were opened" they immediately noticed their nakedness and felt the need to cover up. Not only would they have looked ridiculous, but they would have felt strange and awkward, having never worn clothes before ... if you could call leaves clothes! Later in the story God covers them up and does a much better job. Covering up was a denial of their identity and an attempt to create a new one. The fig leaves were not only a new look, they were a new life.

When we're not sure who we are or even comfortable with our God-given identity, we resort to using everything and anything to cover up the purity of our *naked self*. Before God, the person we were made to be is magnificent and glorious. We don't need leaves or leather to improve the look, He likes us as we really are. The problem is we generally don't. Insecure with ourselves, uncertain of our God, lacking confidence in the truth, we're always under pressure to cover up, disguise or divert people's gaze from who we really are onto the "improved" version we put on display. Can you imagine what God must have thought the first time He saw the glory of His creation covered in leaves? They undoubtedly thought it was an improvement, but God probably thought it an insult. Why cover up with imperfection something He made perfect?!

Are you covering up? I'm not talking now about your body. I, for one, thank God for clothes. I'm one of those people who looks much better with clothes on! I'm talking about *you*, the real, glorious, God-made you. No matter what we use to dress or cover our God-given identity, it can never improve on the original. The devil wants to so confuse us that we'll put multi-layers of stuff on top of our naked self because he knows: the more layers, the less the vibrancy of our lives will shine through and the more unhappy we will become. It's time to leave the leaves on the trees and let your lovely naked self be seen!

Spiritual insecurity

"...and they hid from the LORD God among the trees of the garden."
(Genesis 3:8)

Insecurity, at its most basic, involves a sense of being unsafe. Adam and Eve were used to walking with God in the garden in the cool of the day, but this time, in another new experience, they hid from Him. They hid because they felt unsafe and they felt unsafe because they were uncertain of who they were and of who God was and, more importantly, how He would react. Their uncertainty about themselves produced insecurity in their relationship with God.

Insecurity with others is always a by-product of uncertainty in or with us. When we are insecure in who we are, we will struggle to trust other people. This lack of trust and insecurity will, in turn, produce in us an inferiority which will always have us running for the bushes. When confronted by God as to their behaviour, Adam's response is telling:

"...I was afraid..."

(Genesis 3:10)

But why would he be afraid of his Creator, the One he used to go for walks with?

Adam's personal insecurity, his loss of confidence in his identity, placed him in a precarious position. For the first time in his life he was afraid and he responded by panicking, running and hiding.

Insecurity within our personhood will impact on how we stand before God, how we relate to Him, worship Him and serve Him.

Fear, the fruit of insecurity, will continually get in the way and we'll find ourselves, more often than not, hiding behind a bush instead of standing confidently and boldly in His presence. Adam ran because he wasn't sure. The tragedy of the moment is not so much where he ran, but why he ran.

John declares that it is only the absence of love which gives fear permission to reign. Fear will have easy access to our lives when we are no longer certain of who we are and who God is.[4] Confusion on either or both of these truths will lead inevitably to spiritual insecurity and confirm us as permanent residents of Bushville, on the edge of Eden.

Relational disfunctionality

> *"The woman you put here with me . . . "*
>
> (Genesis 3:12)

Personal vulnerability and spiritual insecurity will quickly lead us to relational disfunctionality. It's only a matter of time before the uncertainty of our experience expresses itself in a need to find an excuse as to why we are the way we are! Picture the scene: Adam approaches God rather sheepishly from behind the trees and the bushes. He tries to stand upright, before his Creator. At that point he realises Eve made a mistake by not including pockets in his first set of clothes, so with nowhere to put his hands, they end up clasped in front of his leaves covering his bits, braced in fear as if about to face the first Divine free-kick in history . . . how embarrassing. What's a man in his position to do? That's it . . . blame the woman! In fact, it could be argued that Adam is blaming both God and the woman: "It was her fault really, but *You* arranged the marriage!"

The harmonious world of Eden now disintegrates into the blame game. "It wasn't me, it was her!" "It wasn't me, it was the serpent!"

"It wasn't me . . ." Sorry mate, you're bottom of the food-chain in this equation, there's no one else to blame, you're it!

Over the years as a leader I've met many people who, for one reason or another, are living lives of insecurity and identity confusion. In their attempt to justify their fig leaves they do the easy thing and blame somebody or something else. "I'm like this because . . ." I don't wish to minimize anyone's pain, for the journeys each of us have made contain factors and influences which undoubtedly have contributed to who we are and where we are. But the challenge for each of us is this: unless and until we take personal responsibility for who we are and where we are going, the blame game is always going to represent the easiest and most attractive option. The problem is, blaming others may excuse us, but it will never change us!

For the first time, a serious fracture appeared between Adam and Eve. Up to this point they had done everything together . . . even down to eating that fruit and sewing those leaves. But now that the spotlight is on and God is applying some pressure to the scenario, Adam cracks and in so doing brings division into his home. Confusion over our identity will do that. If we hate or even dislike ourselves then we're going to find it difficult, if not impossible, to truly like or love other people. If we are confused about ourselves, we'll struggle to trust anyone and if we're unhappy with our lot, we'll rarely take responsibility when there's someone else we can blame . . . usually those within striking distance. All this is a recipe for relational disfunctionality and identity confusion.

Displaced personality

> "So the LORD God banished him from the Garden of Eden to work the ground from which he had been taken."

(Genesis 3:23)

It's better than dying I suppose . . . but is it living? Could anything ever compare to the glory and splendour of Eden, to what they had and who they were? No matter how good this new place looked, it would never be Eden.

Living in the delight of Eden is only possible as we live in the identity of the person God made us and experience the plans for which He has called us. There is an Eden for us all, a place of abundance and joy which comes out of the knowledge of who we are, and produces the security and rest we need to live our lives well. Adam had to get used to the world of weeds and hardship because he forgot too quickly who he was and held too lightly what he had. This is not God's plan for us. He does not want us to be banished from our Eden, living life with furrowed brows and broken hearts. He wants us to experience the freedom and laughter of understanding our God-given identity, an identity that only we were made to own.

God made Adam and Eve in His image to live with Him, reflect Him and serve Him. All of this was sacrificed for something they didn't need in pursuit of an identity they already had. Hustled out of their inheritance, they paid a high price for their mistakes and stand as a lesson to us all. Today the devil is no less zealous in his pursuit of our identities and the destruction of our Eden. He wants no child of God to live in a delightful place. Instead his ambition is that each of us will end up in places of sorrow, regret and hardship. The truth is he cannot steal our identity from us unless we are willing to give it away, but he will use every trick in the book and some that the censors have cut out, to confuse us and lead us to compromise who we know we are. He knows if he succeeds in this quest, there's only one direction we're heading and that's out of Eden.

Notes

1. *Identity Theft, Don't become a Victim,* published by the UK Home Office. www.identitytheft.org.uk.

2. 1 Timothy 2:14.

3. John, J., & Stibbe, M., *A Barrel of Fun,* Monarch Books, 2003, p. 96.

4. 1 John 4:18.

The Born Identity

When the body was pulled from the water the fishermen who rescued him had no idea who the young man was. Two bullet wounds in his back, a few scars and a mysterious pellet extracted from his hip displaying the details of a Swiss bank account distinguished him without identifying him. What further added to the mystery was when the young man was revived, he was suffering from complete memory loss and had no idea who he was. His name was Jason Bourne, a government agent trained to kill, but at that moment, as far as he was aware, he could have been anyone. Through a series of clues, the pellet, the contents of his bank box and the awareness of certain "gifts and talents" he possessed, he began to piece together his life in an attempt to discover the truth of his identity. As the story progresses, it becomes clear that he has to find his identity in order to save his life.[1]

Imagine waking up one day with such memory loss that you can't remember who you are, where you were from or where you were going! Imagine then trying to piece together your identity and the purpose of your life by the "clues" left all around you. I wonder, would we be able to find our way back or would we remain lost and simply assume another identity?

At the end of World War II, more than fifty men emerged from the prison camps of Indochina suffering from amnesia. They could not remember who they were and there were no records to help identify them. Someone suggested the idea that the photographs of the men be displayed in a Parisian newspaper, announcing that these men would appear on the stage of the city's Opera House. The article encouraged anyone who thought they knew the soldiers to come to the Opera House and make a positive identification. According to the story, on the evening in question, the first soldier marched onto the stage and looking out over the audience asked the question, "Does anybody out there know who I am?" [2]

If we are confused about who we are and why we are here, there are clues all around us and, dare I say, even within us, designed by Almighty God to help us find the way. God Himself has given us an unmissable starting point:

> *"For we are God's masterpiece. He has created us anew in Christ Jesus,*
> *so that we can do the good things he planned for us long ago."*
>
> (Ephesians 2:10 NLT)

If we dare to believe the truth contained within this statement, light will begin to invade darkened rooms within our hearts and we will begin to discover the power of our *God-created selves*. Paul's proclamation presents to us an amazing insight, that *who* we are is inextricably linked to *what* we are "called" to do; that our personality is deliberately linked to our purpose and that we should not consider one without the other. We are being encouraged by Paul to step back for a few moments from the minutiae and busyness of demand-driven living and see the bigger picture of our lives. To set our lives in an eternal context, to realise that our beginnings have divine origin and to grasp that our identity and purpose, though not determined in a narrow fatalistic way, has been shaped by God. If we can discover the "who" that He made and the "why" of His preferred purpose, then life, though never easy, can be lived with joyful enthusiasm, humble privilege and purpose-spiced opportunity. As one writer put it, "You were born pre-packed. God looked at your entire life, determined your assignment, and gave you the tools to do the job."[3]

Paul's statement declares the glory of God's intentionality over our lives. This is not something to be feared. Our heavenly Father is not some mad professor experimenting with our lives, hoping for the right results, but with no regard for the "rats" in the lab. Rather it teaches us that at the centre of His immense eternal plan is His love for humanity and with that His attention to detail. He does not see a planet, rather He sees people. He is not interested in conformity, rather He's invested massively in individuality. He's not merely hoping for a useful outcome, rather He's planning for the best ... our best, and He has left nothing to chance, no detail has been missed and everything is in place. All that's left is that we discover who we are and unreservedly engage.

You were born to be the person conceived in the mind of God from eternity past. That's why so much investment is being expended in an attempt to confuse and distract you and perhaps ultimately destroy you. The forces opposed to the magnificence of God's eternal plan understand this powerful and radical truth, that *our identity is connected to our destiny*. What God designed us to do before the earth began is rooted in who God intended us to be. Destroy our God-intended identity and our God-purposed destiny will never see the light of day.

So where can we look for the clues that will help us make this journey of discovery? What information can help us to discover who we are and why we are here?

Look at the Book

Let me remind you again of the words of Paul to the Ephesian church ... and to you!

"For we are God's masterpiece. He has created us anew in Christ Jesus, so that we can do the good things he planned for us long ago."

God's glorious Word contains incredible truth not only about God, but about *you*! If we had no other words from God about who we are than these, we would have enough fuel in the tank to make all the journeys before us. Imagine it, *you* are the workmanship, the masterpiece of God Himself. *You* were created brand new in Christ Jesus and there are works prepared for *you* which only *you* can do. Too many live lives of aimless recklessness because they do not know what God thinks of them or what His book says about them. Too many listen to the wisdom of a so-called enlightened society that judges the value of the human spirit with shallow super-ficiality, discarding those who don't fit the profile, while celebrating a small minority who have achieved the holy grail of success and celebrity. If bought into, such frivolous philosophy dehumanizes the soul, disconnects us from the Divine, and condemns us to a life of hopeless mediocrity, tormented by unrealistic expectations.

Knowledge of the truth produces freedom. As Jesus said, *"Then you will know the truth, and the truth will set you free."*[4] The truth of God's words to us have the power to liberate us from the shackles of other people's opinions and the prison of our own smallness that so often dictates the limitations of our lives. The challenge before us is to have the courage to dive into the Word of God and find what He actually says, and then having discovered it, make a choice to believe it and live it.

Over the years I have met many people who genuinely believe that God is playing "hide and seek" with them when it comes to their identity and purpose. Somehow, He's hidden from them the secret of life and it's their job to find it . . . eventually . . . hopefully. Many of the great religions of the world present a god who waits to be found by us. We have to do the seeking and the searching, and hopefully, at some point, we'll stumble upon the truth. But this is not the God of the Bible, the God who demonstrated Himself through Jesus. Instead He comes searching for us. No other God has worked harder at revealing the mystery of His will to us. He's given us His Word in words and in flesh, so that we wouldn't spend the whole of our lives searching for something that is hidden; rather we would find that which heaven has already revealed.

Look at the Book! It tells us we are made in the image of God (Genesis 1:27), it tells us God has a hope and future for us (Jeremiah 29:10–11), it tells us there is no one in the whole universe like us (Psalm 139:13–14), it tells us we are the apple of God's eye (Deuteronomy 32:10), it tells us we are loved and precious to God (John 3:16) and in the New Testament it tells us approximately ninety-one times that we are "in Christ".[5] Now with just a glance, look what we've discovered! Just think what we might find out about our identity if we have the determination to open it for ourselves and look for the truth that the God of heaven who loves us beyond imagination has already revealed.

The first big clue to your born identity is in the Book, and we need only look. Go on, I dare you!

To be or not to be

"If you are what you ain't, then you ain't what you are!"[6]

"Just be yourself", sounds so simple doesn't it, and yet for many of us it has proved to be an extremely complex thing to do. I was staggered recently by a statistic which stated that as many as twenty-one million people in Britain might be in the wrong job due to a mismatch of their personality and skills with their current employment.[7] I'm not sure about twenty-one million, but from my experience, I know it's true of many. Over the years I've met many people doing jobs they hate because they feel they have no other option, due to educational limitation, their age or financial pressure. These, of course, are factors that cannot be ignored, but the main casualty is the person at the heart of the story who is doing something for which they are not really suited, while missing the purpose for which they were born. As the Bard said: "To thine own self be true . . . "

After speaking at a conference I went into the restaurant for a drink and hopefully some ice-cream. As I took my seat at a table, a gentleman at another table invited my friends and me to join him. In the conversation that followed it became clear this man was an extremely successful businessman, but it also became clear he wasn't very happy about doing what he was doing. After a few minutes of listening to him I interrupted and asked him, "If you could do anything you wanted to, something that you think really reflects the passion of your heart and the gifts you have, what would you do?"

Startled, he looked at me as if no one had ever asked him such a question before. He thought for a moment, then gave me his answer. I replied, "Why don't you do it then?" Maybe I'm missing something, but why do something you hate, when you could do something you love? If your personality passion is people, then why are you working with computers? If you love kids, why work in an old people's home? If you're a leader, then why are you standing in the followers' line?

I know you already know this, but I'll tell you anyway. Life is too short to live the wrong one! The clock is ticking and the older I get the faster it seems to tick. This is not a dress rehearsal for a second go, this is it. We have one shot at making our life on earth count . . . so why waste it trying to be someone you're not, doing something you hate? Money is important, we have to pay the bills, but the purpose of our being has got to be bigger than paying off the mortgage, driving the latest flash car or drawing a pension. There's nothing wrong with any of those things, but let's determine not to allow such small things to govern our eternal existence. As one man put it, "I do not want to die without having lived."

Gillian had a brilliant job in a legal office. Comfortably within her gift range, the job looked after her well. But Gillian started to look inside herself and discovered she was not born to be a legal secretary. She wanted to teach and she loved children. Gillian gave up her job, went to university and graduated as a teacher. It was a risk, people might have thought her crazy, and in the short term there was the pressure of change. Was it worth it? Five minutes with Gillian will convince anyone that this was what she was born to do. Well done, Gillian, for being true to yourself!

The second big clue as to our born identity is in our God-given personality. If being yourself is a clue . . . it begs the question, who are you?

You've got it because you need it

> *"Are you called to help others? Do it with all the strength and energy that God supplies . . . "*
>
> (1 Peter 4:11 LB)

Brennan Manning, one of my favourite authors, encourages us this way. " . . . trust yourself as one entrusted by God with everything you need to live life to the full. Despite our physical cracks, intellectual limitations, emotional impairments, and spiritual fissures, we are providentially equipped to fulfil the unique purpose of our existence."[8]

Did you get that? " . . . providentially equipped to fulfil the unique purpose of our existence." Let's suppose this is true. This means that everything we will ever need to fulfil the God-intended purpose of our lives is already inside us – right now! Discovering what lies within helps us to see who we are and why we are here.

Discovering our God-intended purpose helps us to understand why we are the way we are, and why we've got what we've got.

A common fault of the human condition is comparing ourselves to others and wondering why we are not like them. Life would be so much better if I had the "talent" they have, we think. Maybe, maybe not. What I do know for certain is that when we allow ourselves to fall into the trap of comparison, we not only start to hanker after gifts we haven't got, we also neglect the God-given gifts we do have. We lament our shortcomings instead of celebrating the gifts that reside within us which are just waiting for an excuse to explode onto an unsuspecting world. We spend our precious lives wishing for things we don't need, while ignoring the "pre-packed" blessings of heaven designed to empower us to be and do all we were pre-ordained in Christ to do. So here's my advice: **Stop it!** As Manning suggests, "Any attempt to measure the value of our lives by comparison and contrast to others belittles our gifts and dishonours God by our ungratefulness."[9]

David declares,

> *"For you created my inmost being;*
> *you knit me together in my mother's womb . . .*
> *All the days ordained for me*
> *were written in your book*
> *before one of them came to be."*

(Psalm 139:13, 16)

In other words, in order to do what He's planned for us to do, He's already given us what we need. So, we need to stop looking around and start looking within. It would not be a bad thing to take a blank piece of paper and do an internal audit of our life, specifically highlighting the gifts and talents that (modesty aside) we know reside within us. Every one of us has them. They may not look like those of your father, sister, friend or work-colleague

... but that's a good thing. God has put treasures inside each one of us. They are put there to empower our lives and to enrich our world. We must set our hearts to discover what they are and why they've been given, and we must start right now.

The third big clue to our born identity is the gifts that lie within. They may seem ordinary, routine and natural, but remember, every good gift comes from God our Father, and they come for a reason. In the right context, the ordinary becomes extraordinary, the routine becomes exceptional and the natural gets super as a prefix.

> "Our very existence is one of the never-to-be repeated ways God has chosen to express Himself in space and time." [10]

Holy orders

> *"But when God, who set me apart from birth and called me by his grace, was pleased to reveal his Son in me so that I might preach him among the Gentiles..."*
>
> (Galatians 1:15–16)

Before Paul met Jesus on the Damascus road, he was being what he thought he should be and using his God-given talents as he thought they ought to be used. In accordance with his beliefs, he zealously persecuted the Church and sought to export his religious brand beyond the boundaries of his own nation. Highly intelligent, passionate, missional and courageous, Saul, as he was then called, went on a one man crusade to save the world from the perils of the heretic Jesus and His misguided followers. All that changed the day Jesus knocked him off his horse and changed the direction of his life. As God told Ananias, *"... this man is my chosen instrument to carry my name before the Gentiles and their kings and before the people of Israel"* (Acts 9:15).

Saul, now Paul, is still highly intelligent, passionate, missional and courageous, but now he understands who he is, the gifts he's been given and the God-intended purpose for which they were deposited inside him. The single-minded go-getter now has a new obsession and a new focus for his life. What changed all this? A single holy order from Jesus Himself. The command and call of Christ showed Paul in an instant why he was the way he was and why he had what he had. Suddenly, it all made sense. That's why Paul could conclude that God had set him apart from birth. Technically it wasn't true. Paul had lived many years selfishly pursuing what he thought was right for his life and the best use of his talents. However, when his eyes were opened, he suddenly realised the purpose for his pre-packedness and it all made sense. He now saw God's hand in his life from the beginning and determined to live the rest of his life accordingly.

Paul later said, *"... our goal is to stay within the boundaries of God's plan for us ..."* (2 Corinthians 10:13 NLT). The most important discovery we can make is that our lives do not actually belong to us, they belong to God. Whoever we are and whatever we have has been given by Him and is intended for Him. When we live for ourselves, we live outside the boundaries of God's plan for us and therefore never truly discover who we were really intended to be and the God-intended purpose for which we were put on the earth.

In 1888, Alfred Nobel read his own premature obituary in a French newspaper. It contained the words, "The merchant of death is dead" and had the effect of radically changing his life. Dr Alfred Nobel had invented dynamite and had become extremely rich in the process. As the obituary put it, he "... became rich by finding ways to kill more people faster than ever before". From that moment on Alfred Nobel decided to use his talents and gifts for the betterment of humanity and not for its destruction. On 27th November 1895, at the Swedish-Norwegian Club in Paris, he signed his last will and testament, setting aside the bulk of his estate for the establishment of the Nobel Prizes. After his death in 1896, it is estimated he left 31 million kronor to fund the prizes.[11]

Nobel's life changed when he saw his life from a different perspective. The change of view radically affected how he lived and how he used the "talents" given to him from above.

The fourth big clue to discovering our born identity is seeing our life from God's perspective, hearing what God says about us, allowing Him to show us why He made us the way we are and why He gave us what we have. To ignore the God factor is to miss the greatest key of all. We must open up our hearts to hear what He has to say about us.

As John Henry Newman put it,

> "Fear not that your life shall come to an end, but rather that it shall never have a beginning."

Notes

1. 2002 movie entitled *The Bourne Identity*, starring Matt Damon, based loosely on the 1980 spy fiction thriller of the same name, written by Robert Ludlum. Three years and three movies later, he discovers his real name is David Webb . . . I think I like Jason Bourne better!
2. Campolo, T., *Let Me Tell You a Story*, Word, 2000, p. 183.
3. Lucado, M., *Cure for the Common Life*, W Publishing Group, 2005, p. 13.
4. John 8:32.
5. NIV Anglicised version.
6. David Crystal, *As They Say in Zanzibar*, Collins, 2006, p. 36. An America proverb.
7. Statistic given by Angelina Bennett, an occupational psychologist, in an interview on BBC Radio 2 on 29th March 2007.
8. Brennan Manning, *Ruthless Trust*, HarperCollins, 2000, pp. 145–146.
9. Manning, *Ruthless Trust*, p. 144.
10. Manning, *Ruthless Trust*, p. 147.
11. www.wikipedia.org. 31 million kronor is estimated to be worth approximately 103,931,888 USD in 2007.

CHAPTER 3

Don't Be a Dolly

Although her birth was not announced to the world until February 1997, Dolly was born on Friday 5th July 1996. She was one of millions of sheep born that year in the United Kingdom, but she was different, because Dolly was a clone. Originally code-named 6LL3 (it's got a certain ring to it don't you think?), she was given the name Dolly by one of the stockmen who helped with her birth. Having been cloned from a mammary cell, he thought it fitting to name her after Dolly Parton! (If you don't get that, ask your doctor). Now for the technical bit. The technique used to produce Dolly is known as "somatic cell nuclear transfer". This is when the nucleus of a donor cell (in this case taken from a six-year-old Finn Dorset ewe), is placed in a de-nucleated ovum. The donor nucleus is then reprogrammed by the ovum and this develops into an embryo. Dolly was the first mammalian clone produced from an adult somatic cell.[1]

Due to a progressive lung disease, scientists at the Roslin Institute decided that Dolly, the world's most famous sheep, should be put down. She was put out of her misery at 3.30 pm on Friday, 14th February, 2003. However, if you're desperate to see her, Dolly's stuffed remains are displayed at Edinburgh's Royal Museum in Scotland.

Even though Dolly was a genetic copy, a clone, it could also be argued she was unique. According to the dictionary definition, uniqueness points to being "the only one, having no equal or parallel". However, what cannot be said of Dolly is that she was an original. Although she had a name and a life and even reproduced her own lambs by natural means, Dolly was a copy of an original, and therefore could never be an original herself.

Once, while travelling in Asia, a friend of mine became very excited about the prospect of visiting the local market because of some of the goods available there. Not being much of a shopper, I left him to it and on one of our free afternoons, he shopped while I sunned! When he returned from his expedition he could hardly contain himself as he hurriedly displayed his goods. "Look," he said, "I got three Rolex watches for $10US! They wanted $5 for one, but I got three for $10. What a bargain!"

Now, I've never owned a Rolex watch, but I know they are usually a bit more expensive than $5, and in all my years I've never seen Rolex promote a 3-for-2 offer! Not wishing to burst my friend's bubble, I nevertheless tried to point out to him what seemed to me like an obvious fact. "You bought three watches, but they're not Rolex!" He looked at me as if I had just confessed to being the antichrist, but I pressed on. "They look like Rolex, but the truth is they're not, they are just cheap copies ... and they don't come close to the original." Needless to say, none of his "genuinely copied" Rolex watches came my way.

I saw an advertisement once that warned, "Beware of expensive imitations". If you are prepared to make a serious pilgrimage with God you'll discover He's not into imitations, copies or clones. He specializes and rejoices in originality. Though it is in some ways the ultimate compliment to any original that someone would want to copy it, God has never and will never stoop to clone anything or anyone. He continually invests Himself into designing and releasing originality. Even a casual glance at the creation story in the book of Genesis shows God's creative genius in imagining such a universe and making it reality. Look at the regal beauty of a giraffe, the slumbering wobble of a hippopotamus and the magnificent markings of the tiger and you see absolute originality. Who in their wildest dreams would have conceived that long neck, those gaping jaws and such breathtaking artistry? But you don't need to go to a zoo or on safari to see what you consider to be creative originality, you can see it right now. All you have to do is find a mirror and look in it. Stop looking at the flaws or the flab, just for a moment look at you and remember this thought: "You are the only you that has ever been, that currently is, or that ever will be." It's your face, your space and your life. You're not a copy or an expensive imitation, you're a fully licensed original and God loves you!

Enough of the mirror for a moment, now look into another mirror with me, the Bible. Read these powerful words with your mind focused and your heart open.

> "For you created my inmost being;
>> you knit me together in my mother's womb.
> I praise you because I am fearfully and wonderfully made;
>> your works are wonderful,
>> I know that full well.
> My frame was not hidden from you
>> when I was made in the secret place.
> When I was woven together in the depths of the earth,
>> your eyes saw my unformed body.
> All the days ordained for me
>> were written in your book
>> before one of them came to be."

(Psalm 139:13–16)

If chapter 2 was an insight into God's intentionality over our lives, then this chapter is a celebration of God's commitment to originality. The verses from Psalms demonstrate high levels of divine investment into ensuring that every person reading these words is doing so not as a copy or a sweat-shop imitation, but as an original – one of a kind. Though you are similar to those around you, you're also very different. Though there's a commonality of experience, you're also unique. Though you might be categorized in a certain demographic or sociological group, you'll always stand out from the crowd. Though the government may know you as a number, Almighty God, the Originator of originality, knows you by name!

Let's look a bit closer at these verses. I hope to unearth for you some remarkable and priceless jewels. I want to highlight some amazing truths that give us insight about our originality.

Originality in personality

I remember the first time I saw my oldest daughter. She was only about twelve weeks old and still in her mother's womb. Dawn and I were on holiday in America and due to suspected food poisoning, Dawn found herself in hospital, on a drip and having an unscheduled ultrasound. As I looked at the screen and marvelled at the tiny human being moving around oblivious of all the fuss, I was overwhelmed with a sense of awe, that somehow I had, along with my wife, played a part in creating this original human being. Elaina was born in 1993 and since then has been joined by Simeon and Beth-Anne. Amazingly, although they are all from the same gene pool, each displays a distinct personality and their own aspirations. How is it possible that three human beings produced by the same parents and living in the same environment can be so different? Here's another amazing thought. Every second approximately three babies are born somewhere in the world. That's 259,200 per day, and according to the genius of God's creative design, every one of them is unique.[2]

It would be easy to reduce the quest for such an answer to a matter of biology, psychology or genetics. Although I respect and appreciate so many of the advancements in these arenas that have helped inform us of the mystery that is humanity, I want us to gaze for a moment at this mystery through the lens of theology. Verses 13–15 have some incredible things to say about God's involvement in the formative development of our personhood. The Psalmist suggests that who we are is not merely a result of genetics, but also of the genius of God Himself, at work in us. Within these verses there are three pictures which give us a clue to the originality of our personality.

The first picture is in verse 13:

> *"For you created my inmost being;*
> *you knit me together in my mother's womb."*

As a boy, I used to read the King James Version of the Bible and this verse read,

> *"For thou hast possessed my reins . . . "*

It took me a while to work it out, but I discovered the word translated "reins" literally means "kidneys", which came to denote the inward part of a person, their soul, the seat of their desires, their affections and passions. It wasn't that God had a particular speciality in kidneys, but rather He specifically invested in "possessing" or making my inner being – my personality. The Psalmist suggests that the innermost recesses of our beings have been constituted by God.

The second picture is in verse 14:

> *"I praise you because I am fearfully and wonderfully made;*
> *your works are wonderful,*
> *I know that full well."*

The literal translation here could read, "I am distinguished by fearful things; that is, by things in my creation which are suited to inspire awe." David saw himself as "distinguished" or "separated" from among the other works of creation and even amongst other human beings. There is no hint of any sense of superiority, but simply that he saw himself as distinct, unique.

The third picture is in verse 15:

> *"My frame was not hidden from you*
> *   when I was made in the secret place.*
> *When I was woven together in the depths of the earth . . . "*

The word "woven" can literally be translated "embroidered". The Hebrew word means "to deck with colour, to weave with threads of various colours". The emphasis is not merely on the colours being woven in, but on the intricacy of the weaving and even the skill of the weaver. As one commentator put it, this is a " . . . beautiful figure for the complicated and elaborately-contrived texture of the human body."[3]

These three beautiful pictures demonstrate to us two truths. The first truth is that God is intimately involved in the formation and development of every human *being*. Just as genetics has a role, so does God. To remove Him from His domain of originality not only does a great disservice to the Creator God, but it robs each of us of a special uniqueness that has it origins in the divine, not just the human. We are challenged to enter into our biology through the doorway of theology.

The second truth is that you and I are one of a kind, completely original in every way. How many times have you heard it said of someone, "They broke the mould when they made him . . . " Well, that isn't just the territory of an eccentric or a dynamic charismatic, that applies to us all. Each of us has been made from an original mould. None of us are copies or clones or second-thought imitations. We, you and I, are one of a kind, moulded by the hand of God and engineered to unique specifications. It amazes me that society and organized religion expends a lot of energy trying to get everyone to look and be the same, when God has invested colossal energy to make sure each of us are different. God doesn't want you to be a Dolly, He wants you to be you.

Originality in purpose

Anyone who knows me is aware of my legendary do-it-yourself skills. My most repeated prayer is "God, please don't let it break." I'm not very good at building or fixing things. I know God understands this, because He's given me wonderful friends (including a DIY savvy wife) who over the years have helped keep my house standing. I remember assisting my father-in-law with some jobs in my house (combining DIY and in-laws is not always a good thing), when he asked me to pass him a Philips screwdriver. I dutifully handed him a screwdriver. He looked at it in disgust and said, a little more forcibly, "A Philips screwdriver!" It turns out that not all screwdrivers are the same. I thought a screwdriver was a screwdriver . . . oh, no. I won't bore you with the technical terms, but there's a lot of different types. The Philips screwdriver was designed to fit a specific style of screw and without it, that particular job just wouldn't have got done.

Verse 16 says,

> " . . . *All the days ordained for me*
> *were written in your book,*
> *before one of them came to be.*"

We've touched on this verse already in chapter 2, in a slightly different context, but it's worth looking at again. Part of our originality is the purpose for which we are "called" or designed.

Though I'm not so good at DIY, I'm really good at other things, such as . . . just give me a minute . . . it's coming . . . I'll get back to that later. The trick is to realise that just because I can't repair the central heating system does not mean I'm useless. I need to find the stuff I'm good at, the things I was designed to fit and then do the best I possibly can. Okay, I've thought of something. The guy who makes fixing my central heating look easy might hyperventilate at the prospect of standing in front of hundreds of people and leaders and teaching them the Word of God, but I love that. I was born to do that. I find that "easy" to do. I'm not saying I'm the best in the world at it, but for me, it fits. I'd rather do that than ever touch a screwdriver again.

This is what David is driving at in this verse. He is not pointing to some fatalistic view of God's purpose for us, but rather that God has a preferred purpose for us, a pre-designed best for each of us, that when discovered brings that moment of "click" . . . it fits like it was made to fit. The Bible declares that in every human being there is an originality of purpose, a book with a unique story inside, written only for us and waiting to be opened and read by us. Only you can live the life designed for you and only you can do what God designed you to do. God has written a lot of books. Perhaps it is time you got yours off the shelf and not only read it, but lived it. God doesn't want you to be a Dolly, a copy of someone else's expectations or dream. He doesn't want you to live the life that others think you should live (although it's good to get as much wisdom from friends as possible), but He wants you to live the original life He planned for you. Look inward at the gifts God has given you, and then look upward for the purpose for which they were given.

Originality in price

> "How precious to me are your thoughts, O God!"
>
> (Psalm 139:17)

Today you can hang a Van Gough, a Constable or a Bacon (that's the painter not the food) in your living room for less than £100, yet the originals would cost hundreds of thousands of pounds, even millions. To the untrained eye they look identical, but not to the expert who knows the difference between the original and a copy. You don't have to be an expert of course. The chances are if you bought a Van Gough from Tesco or Walmart, it's probably a copy. The value of the painting is not simply determined by the beauty or intricacy of the image, but by the fact that one has been touched by the trembling hands of the artist, the other by the sweaty palms of a photocopier technician.

The reason we are so precious and valuable is because we have been touched by the hands of the Originator of originality Himself. Somehow, as we were cooking in our mother's womb, Almighty God climbed into that small space and got involved. He put things within us that add up to more than the sum of our genetic parts, and He breathed into us a spirit that yearns and calls for the eternal and remains unsatisfied by the fleeting highs of a material world. Many reading this book have been battered and scarred by life and under the bruising it's easy to miss the genius of the original and the magnificence of that potential. After a few knocks and disappointments it's easier to accept the drivel of *Dolly*wood. Maybe we're not that original after all, we begin to think, maybe we're meant to be part of the crowd, a fairly decent but inexpensive copy that will grace the walls of some bland suburban home. If we give in to this, not only will our world, our families, our marriages and our churches, the places that long for and need our originality, be impoverished, but we will join the band of the living dead, those who have decided that originality is too expensive a dream and too costly a lifestyle. Herein lies the trap within the world of the copy. Though it doesn't cost much, it's actually not worth anything! Living a copy, imitation, Dolly-like existence will keep the costs down for us all, but what we end up with at the end of the journey will be of no value at all. This is the glory of this passage. The theology contained in these verses wrenches us away from a hopeless, humanistic estimation of our past, present and future, and entice us towards a truth that has the power to propel us into a new orbit of thinking and an enhanced level of living.

Amy was born into a loving home and it soon became apparent she had the most gorgeous brown eyes. However, Amy wanted blue eyes, not brown, and as a young child prayed earnestly to God to give her the blue eyes she so desperately wanted. One particular night she prayed, sure that God would answer her prayers, and when she woke the next morning, she rushed to the mirror to see and there staring at her . . . you guessed it, were two beautiful brown eyes. Many years later, Amy found herself in India confronted with a hideous crime against children who were being forced to be temple prostitutes. The only way to rescue them was to infiltrate the culture and go "under-cover". As she prepared to embark on this dangerous mission (one which would bring her much criticism), she put on the Indian sari and stained the exposed areas of her skin with coffee powder, so as to enter the places where foreign women were prohibited. Had she possessed blue eyes instead of brown, she would have been recognized immediately as a foreigner, whatever her disguise, and her plans would have been destroyed. Amy Carmichael, the darling of Dohnavur, rescued a generation as an original, not a copy. Had God given in to her request and given her blue eyes, she would have become an inferior clone not an amazing "brown-eyed" original. Instead, God mercifully spared her from a life as a Dolly and empowered her to live the life of Amy. As a result, millions of people all around the world are the richer for it.

God will never stoop to cloning, He's only interested in originality. You are not a clone, a copy or a cheap and nasty imitation, you are an original masterpiece, shaped, moulded and designed by the Originator of originality Himself. So, for God's sake and yours, don't be a Dolly – be yourself!

Notes

1. Wikipedia – May 2007.
2. http://www.worsleyschool.net/socialarts/world/population.html. Check out the world counter for yourself.
3. Jamieson, Fausset and Brown Commentary of the Bible.

Define or Be Defined

When I was preparing to leave home as a seventeen-year-old, my mother offered me some invaluable advice. Her departing son stood six foot one inches tall, while she, after just over fifty years of growing at that time, stood at an intimidating four foot eleven. For eye-to-eye contact to occur something had to give. You guessed it ... that something was me. My red-blooded Irish mother took hold of me and pulled me towards her. Then she said something I shall never forget: "Wherever you go and whatever you do, remember who you are and where you came from." Since that day, I've had the joy of travelling to numerous nations and doing things I never dreamed possible for a "wee lad" from Belfast. Many times I've been left breathless by the beauty all around me, challenged by the expectations placed upon me, and on occasions intoxicated by the glory given to me. But the simple words of my mother spoken all those years ago have remained a constant maxim in the defining and most memorable experiences of my life.

The older we grow and the further we journey, the more complicated life seems to get. That which seemed simple as a young person starting out on an adventure of service for God can somehow become confused by pressure, pleasure and prestige. If we are not careful, we find ourselves doing things we never really wanted to do and being someone we swore we'd never become. We promise to be true to the dream that beats within us and to never compromise on the purity of our passion for a God-shaped personality, but then life just happens and before we know it, we're firmly ensconced in the middle of the road – we have become a thoroughly nice, convictionless person, happy to be one of the crowd.

I sat with a broken-hearted young man as he wept compromise-filled tears, having, in his own opinion, sold out on his personhood and the purpose he once passionately espoused. Over and over again he kept saying, "How did this happen to me? How did I get here?" It's too easy to judge such a story. However, any serious pilgrim who has endeavoured to make their journey will confess to the subtle and alluring temptation that on occasion encouraged them to "forget" the defining origins that have shaped their identity and destiny. Such pilgrims have earned the right to teach us a powerful life principle: *if we do not define ourselves, someone or something else will define us.* They have learned that a clear understanding of identity will prohibit others from presuming they have the right to define who we are.

When Aleksander Kudajczyk sat down to play the piano in the chapel of Glasgow University he had no idea of the impact his talent was about to have. His musical exploits were captured on webcam and pretty soon staff right around the campus were logging on to listen. Chaplaincy secretary Joan Keenan said, "I couldn't believe it – he was playing the most amazing music." Aleksander started learning the piano when he was four years old and was a professional musician in Poland before trying a make a new life for himself in the UK. So why all the fuss? Mr Kudajczyk was a janitor at the time, cleaning the corridors of the University. Clearly folks were shocked and surprised that a man normally seen using a mop could also play enchanting music. Who would have thought that the economic migrant cleaning the toilets had it in him to play Chopin at Glasgow's West End Festival?[1]

Daniel, Hananiah, Mishael and Azariah faced a serious challenge. It was their generation that experienced the bitterness of enslavement and a captivity-filled future. With the removal of their freedom came the threat to everything they were and all they knew. The book of Daniel is remarkable for so many different reasons and thousands of pages have already been filled with its significance. However, at its most simplistic level, I believe the message at the heart of the book is the battle for identity. It contains the story of a people (highlighted through the experiences of these four individuals) whose way of life and distinctive culture is under threat from a super-power intent on eradicating or assimilating all opposition for the greater glory of the empire. When Daniel and his three friends were "invited" into the palace, the easiest thing in the world would have been to go with the flow, embrace the brave new world before them and *forget* where they had come from and who they were.

In this chapter I wish to draw your attention to three stories involving one or all of these four young men. These exciting stories have, at their core, truths that not only touch issues of nationhood and cultural distinctiveness, but demonstrate the power of identity, intertwined with images of community, spirituality, loyalty, courage and integrity. In each episode the identity of these young Hebrew men is threatened, yet not only do we see their God-given identity remain intact, but this fact becomes the key component through which they conquer the seemingly irresistible forces around them. Having defined themselves they refuse to be defined by anything or anybody else. The heroics in these stories are not only seen in their defiant dietary requirements, their courage in the fierce furnace or the calm assurance in the lions' den – these actions are *merely* the outworking of an even greater heroism, that of staying true to who they were. Perhaps they understood that had they compromised their identity and life, they would at best be dead men walking. They resisted all attempts to define them because they had already defined themselves.

Knowing who they were encouraged them to *"Stand out"*

Look at Daniel 1:7:

> *"The chief official gave them new names: to Daniel, the name Belteshazzar; to Hananiah, Shadrach; to Mishael, Meshach; and to Azariah, Abednego."*

This was meant to be the beginning of the end for the Hebrew identity of Daniel and his three friends. In his desire to subjugate those nations already under the reach of his mighty empire, Nebuchadnezzar instigated a process designed to assimilate the cream of each people group, in this case the Hebrews, into the heart of Babylonian culture. The first few verses of Daniel's record outline how he intended to do this. Ashpenaz, the chief of his court officials, was given clear instructions. He was to pick the best young men of royal blood he could find (v. 4), relocate them into the palace precinct (v. 3), teach them the language and literature of Babylon (v. 4), feed them with the food of Babylon (v. 5), and train them for three years to serve the king (v. 5).

At the beginning of the process, each of the young men is given a new name – a Babylonian name. The giving of a new name was a mark of dominion and authority. It was customary for the conqueror to impose new names on his slaves. As Ashpenaz gave these young men their new names he was reinforcing, if there had been any doubt, that they were "owned" men, no longer Hebrews, but citizens and servants of Babylon! What is interesting is that each of the Hebrew names these young men had, meant something, as did their Babylonian names. These imposed names, were not just labels but statements.

Daniel's name can mean, "God is my judge or banner", but Belteshazzar means, "A prince or treasure of Bel". Bel was the chief god of the Babylonians.

Hananiah's name means, "The Lord has favoured or is gracious", whereas Shadrach means, "The inspiration of the sun".[2]

Mishael's name means, "He who comes from God", while Meshach means, "He who belongs to the goddess Sheshach".

Azariah's name means, "The Lord helps or is my helper", however, Abednego means, "The slave or servant of Nego". He was the second most prominent god of the Babylonians.

These imposed names were not merely Babylonian labels, rather they were statements of intent and ownership, designed to realign the identity of these young men away from their history, their culture and more importantly – their God! Each of their original names is directly linked to the God they serve. Therefore, it is no coincidence that their new names are crafted to link who they are to a new spiritual power. Perhaps Nebuchadnezzar understood that their identity was rooted in their relationship with God. Break this connection, he thought, and cause them to let go of the God they serve, and hardly any effort will be required to reshape these men into good Babylonian citizens.

Look at verse 8, it's incredibly interesting;

> *"But Daniel resolved not to defile himself with the royal food and wine, and he asked the chief official for permission not to defile himself this way."*

"But Daniel..." we read. It doesn't say, "But Belteshazzar..." This is a sign of things to come throughout the book. Daniel responds to the challenges facing him and does so from a clear understanding of his identity and his relationship with God. Throughout the book, the name Daniel is referred to sixty-nine times, whereas Belteshazzar has a mere ten references. What's striking about these ten references is that not once do we see Daniel use it of himself. Maybe that's why, within the Bible, the title of the book in which these events are recorded, reads in simplistic defiance, *Daniel!*

The outcome of their defiance was twofold. After a ten-day period of not eating Babylonian food "... *they looked healthier and better nourished than any of the young men who ate the royal food*" (Daniel 1:15). After three years of training they stood out from the crowd in more ways than one.

> *"In every matter of wisdom and understanding ... he* [the king] *found them ten times better than all the magicians and enchanters in his whole kingdom."*
>
> (Daniel 1:20)

Remaining true to their identity encouraged them to stand out, when it would have been much easier to take their new names, eat the food and mingle with the crowd. They refused to give the dominant culture around them permission to impose a new identity upon them. Though good servants of Babylon, they remained Hebrews at heart. They never forgot who they were or where they came from!

What does this teach us? *If you don't define you, someone or something else will define you!*

Knowing who you are empowers you to resist all attempts from those around you to put you in whatever box they believe you fit. Sometimes the observations and intentions of others can be sincere and correct, but many times they can be wrong. If you're going to live with you for the rest of your life, it would be a good idea to know who you are. Life in its most routine will exert pressure as it prods and squeezes your identity. The only means of resisting this pressure is knowing who you are.

Knowing who they were empowered them to "*Stand up*"

As can be the tendency with all dictator super-power types, they start believing their own propaganda. Babylon had spread across the earth and under Nebuchadnezzar was reaching the zenith of its power. That's when the king decided that a monument celebrating his greatness should be commissioned. Modesty was not the dominant factor when an image made of gold, some 90 feet high and 9 feet wide, was placed on the plain of Dura. The big statue was one thing, but then the king decided that when a certain signal was given, everyone had to stop what they were doing and bow down to the image of gold. Those refusing would face the consequences by being immediately thrown into a blazing furnace!

Three officials in particular are targeted for special measures. Hananiah, Mishael and Azariah (although their Babylonian names are used in this context), refuse to bow. What makes this more embarrassing for the king, is that they are influential government officials themselves, not just members of the masses. Where was Daniel I hear you say? There are two theories as to why Daniel isn't mentioned in this story. The first is that he wasn't present at the time. Almost twenty years has passed since chapter 1 and it might be that Daniel was in some remote part of the empire at this stage. The second is that Daniel did indeed defy the king by not bowing, but it was prudent to deal with lesser officials first before getting to Daniel. For the actual answer, I suggest you ask Daniel when you see him in heaven.

Faced with the prospect of a brutal death, it is interesting to note the response of the three:

"O Nebuchadnezzar, we do not need to defend ourselves before you in this matter. If we are thrown into the blazing furnace, the God we serve is able to save us from it, and he will rescue us from your hand, O king. But even if he does not, we want you to know, O king, that we will not serve your gods or worship the image of gold you have set up."

(Daniel 3:16–18)

Their defiance was on the basis of their faith and in their identification with Him: *"the God we serve"*. This was not an act of rebellion to the king, for their track record showed that these men had been loyal and faithful servants since entering the service of the king. Rather, these young men were standing up because they had something worth standing up for. They were willing to die because they had something worth living for. Even after twenty years in Babylon, enjoying the fruit of a good and prosperous lifestyle, they still had not forgotten who they were or where they were from. Defined in the context of their faith and their relationship with God, they had not moved one inch from these moorings and remained as committed and defiant as the first day they arrived in Babylon.

Many look at this story and focus on the heroism within the flames, but for me the most heroic thing they did is not seen in their preparedness to die (though this is amazing), but rather in their courage to live for a great cause knowing clearly their own identity. If they died they would die true to themselves, and if they lived, they would live true to themselves!

When the miracle occurred and the three men stood alive and untouched by the flames (with a fourth person who looked like "the son of the gods"), the king addressed them in a very specific way, *"Shadrach, Meshach and Abednego, servants of the Most High God, come out! Come here!"* (Daniel 3:26). He called them as he saw them: not as citizens of Babylon or as his royal officials, but as servants of the Most High God. This was who they were! This is why they stood out and this is why now they emerged from the flames unscathed.

What does this teach us? *When you know who you are, you can create your own flow and not just go with someone else's.*

You will only go with someone else's flow when you're not strong enough to create your own. If you do go with their flow, it should always be because you want to or you've deemed it a good idea, not because there is no alternative! It could be argued that today there is more emphasis on and more celebration of the individual than ever before, and yet the same old challenge of conforming to the crowd remains. Whether it's faith or fashion, cars or homes, the pressure to conform, to be like everyone else, is huge. And all of us, in one form or another, have given in to the flow, concluding it's easier to go with it than resist. But when you know who you are, you live the life you were meant to live, and as a result you will automatically start creating your own flow. If you stand up on the inside, you'll be able to stand up on the outside.

Knowing who he was enabled Daniel to *"Stand firm"*

A new super-power now reigns. Babylon has crumbled from within and the Persians took full advantage. Darius is now in charge of the kingdom of Babylon. Daniel is one of the top three administrators in the kingdom, in a position of influence and power. The political opponents of Daniel were clearly unhappy with him and tried to find ways by hook or by crook of getting him out. However, in an attempt to dig their dirt, they were left totally frustrated:

> *"They could find no corruption in him, because he was trustworthy and neither corrupt nor negligent."*
>
> (Daniel 6:4)

Another plan was hatched, this time around one issue on which they knew he would not compromise. Though he had journeyed far, Daniel had not forgotten who he was or where he had come from. Every day, three times a day, he got down on his knees, faced Jerusalem, prayed and gave thanks to God. A new decree, which the king had been tricked into signing, forbade anyone from praying to any god or man, except the king, for a thirty-day period. But Daniel prayed *"... just as he had done before"* (Daniel 6:10) and willingly walked into the trap set by his opponents.

Under pressure to compromise and hold back, Daniel stood firm and continued to do what he had always done, because that's who he was. His prayers weren't the random actions of a religious fanatic with a death wish; rather, this was a man confident in who he was, at rest in his faith and unwilling to let go of who he was and what he held dear for political expedience or short-term gain. Doing what he had always done could cost Daniel his position, his wealth, his influence and his life. But he did it anyway and as a result he ended up in a lions' den.

After a restless night the king rushed to see what had happened to Daniel. His words are interesting:

> *"When he came near the den, he called to Daniel in an anguished voice, 'Daniel, servant of the living God, has your God, whom you serve continually, been able to rescue you from the lions?'"*

> (Daniel 6:20)

Note that the king calls him by his Hebrew name and makes three direct links between Daniel and his God. Darius had done everything in his power to keep Daniel out of the lions' den, and of all those around the man of God, he shows the greatest insight into who Daniel actually is. Darius links the identity of Daniel with the God he serves and understands that the two things are inseparable.

The words of Darius' decree issued after this incident are simply breathtaking:

> *"I issue a decree that in every part of my kingdom people must fear and reverence the God of Daniel.*
>
> *For he is the living God*
>   *and he endures forever;*
> *his kingdom will not be destroyed,*
>   *his dominion will never end.*
> *He rescues and he saves;*
>   *he performs signs and wonders*
>   *in the heavens and on the earth.*
> *He has rescued Daniel*
>   *from the power of the lions."*

(Daniel 6:26–27)

What does this teach us? *Others can get it if we don't lose it!*

Darius got it and extravagantly decreed it, because Daniel never for a second even looked like losing it. Your identity isn't just important for you, it's important for the world you connect to and engage with. As we'll see later in this book, your world needs the real you to show up. When the real you doesn't show, an inferior you deputises, and when that happens, people never get to see what they should. Had Daniel rolled over on his identity or for expedience let go of who he was, Darius would never have glimpsed the glory of Daniel's God or the power of uncompromising identity. Your office needs you. Your gym needs you. Your class needs you. Make sure *you* turn up, and not someone else who looks like you.

Daniel never forgot who he was or where he had come from. Though he served under two super-powers, his identity remained intact. Empowered and emboldened by this truth, he along with his friends *stood out, stood up* and *stood firm* when many would have long since crumbled and become one of the crowd. They were able to resist being defined by others because they defined themselves.

As my wee mummy said:

> "Wherever you go and whatever you do, remember who you are and where you came from."

Notes _____

1. www.bbc.co.uk/news – 28th June 2007.
2. This is the hardest of the Babylonian names to get a conclusively clear meaning on.

What's in a Name?

Names are very important, just ask John Wayne. The iconic American movie star filled the silver screen in films such as *She Wore a Yellow Ribbon*, *The Searchers*, *The Quiet Man* (one of my wife's favourites), *The Sands of Iwo Jima*, *The Alamo* and, of course, unforgettably in *True Grit*. Who could forget the one-eyed, usually intoxicated Marshall, Rooster J. Cogburn? However, I'm not sure his testosterone-filled frame, distinctive walk and unmistakeable voice would have sat well with the name *Marion*! That's right, Marion. Wayne was originally named Marion Robert Morrison. It was later changed to Marion Michael Morrison (like that helps) after his parents decided to call his younger brother Robert! With all due respect to the Marions of the world, I'm glad *The Duke* changed his name.

It's hard to believe that Reginald Kenneth Dwight has had a four-decade music career. He's sold more than 250 million albums worldwide, as well as hundreds of millions of singles, making him one of the most successful artists of all time. "But I've never heard of him," I hear you say. What about if we use his stage name, Elton John? If nothing else, Elton John is easier to get on an album cover than Regin . . . !

Okay, here's a little quiz for you. See if you can guess the name behind the names: Harry Rodger Webb? Brian Warner? Paul

David Hewson? Curtis James Jackson III? Cheryl Sarkisian LaPierre? Diego de la Vega? Edson Arantes do Nascimento? [1]

How did you do? If you got them all, I'm impressed and might want to suggest you get out a little more. Before you go, however, try this final teaser: who was Grigori Yefimovich Novykh? [2]

Names are important. They are not just convenient labels by which we are known, they can influence how we see ourselves, how we view our world and even how others address us. In the Bible, names usually carried great significance. A name might reflect the circumstances of a person's birth, the attitude of their parents, the aspirations and ambitions of their future, the promises of God for them, or even the condition of their nation at the time of their birth. Names were not given lightly or changed easily, because names were not merely a matter of identification, but rather of *identity*. The Bible teaches us that names have the power to define individuals, places and nations, placing huge significance on the names we give and those we're prepared to accept. As we've already seen in the previous chapter, those entrusted with the responsibility of naming, whether they know it or not, are also given the power to define. It is interesting for example that throughout the Bible, the only person we see naming God is God Himself and that one of His Ten Commandments discourages us from messing in any way with His name. This isn't just because there is something innately holy about His name, but rather because His name is inextricably linked to who He is.

As we journey through the Scriptures we see numerous examples of naming and defining providing us with insights which may assist us in discovering the person we were intended to be.

Named by beginnings?

Sometimes the name we start life with is not the name we'll finish with and our beginnings do not always reflect our end. Where we came from does not determine where we are going, or put another way, our history does not determine our destiny. The Bible shows us some remarkable examples of men and women who started life with one name and finished with another. Their name change often reflected a life change. In essence the dimensions of their lives so radically altered that their names could not remain the same.

Abram, which means "high or exalted father" finished his life with the name Abraham, which means "father of a great multitude or many nations".

Sarai, which means "lady or princess" finished her life with the name Sarah, which means "princess of a multitude".

Jacob, which means "one who supplants, undermines … a deceiver", finished his life with the name Israel, which means "one who prevails with God".

Simon, which means "one who hears or obeys", finished his life with the name Peter, which means "rock".

Each of these examples deserves individual attention which this chapter does not allow, but collectively they teach us powerful principles.

Firstly, the new names were given by God. We'll return to this theme by the end of the chapter, but suffice to say, this demonstrates God intervening into the historical origin of those in question, imposing new meaning and identity on the individuals. Secondly, the new names had a meaning which superseded their old names. In each case the new meaning completely eclipsed the former in a significant way. Thirdly, the new names signified a new purpose and direction for each of those named.

For some people in certain cultures, this can be a literal challenge. When someone tells me their name from another culture, I nearly always ask them what their name means. Over the years in my travels I have encountered people with names (once translated into English) such as "Unloved", "Burden" and

"Weak/Small". My challenge in those moments is to resist the urge to give them a new name there and then! On the other hand, I've met people whose names mean "Hope", "Promise" and "Princess". That's better. In some cases there may be a case for literally changing your name, especially if it no longer reflects the philosophy of your life.

For most reading this book this may not apply. However, the principle still holds. The purpose and dream God has for each one of us will always be bigger than the dream we think we have for ourselves. He wants us to go higher and further than we inevitably think we can. The expectations with which we started our lives, the starter names that have sought to define who we are, or the place we're supposed to fill, may no longer adequately describe that which God is now calling us to.

Ironically, in the economy of God, the name we finish with was inside us from the very beginning, it simply took God's love to call it out of us. Abraham was always inside Abram. Sarah lived dormant within Sarai for many years. Israel was bursting to escape from the limitations of Jacob, and Simon was a rock from his mother's womb. God wants to call you by a new name. He longs to call from you the greatness that is within. If He challenges you, don't be afraid to change the name you were born or started with, for that name as nice as it is, may not suit you; it may not reflect you and it may not fit where and what you are right now.

Named by experience?

Throughout the Bible there are examples of names reflecting experiences, whether negative or positive. Here are some examples:

Seth was named by Eve and his name means "appointed or substitute". He got this name as a direct result of the murder of Abel by Cain. Eve named her third son and saw him as a replacement for a lost child.[3]

Isaac was named by his father Abraham and his name means "laughter". Through Isaac's birth, God brought laughter into Sarah's life. Years of waiting for a son now burst forth into joy and this is reflected in the name of her first son.[4]

Joseph had two sons while in Egypt. He called his first son Manasseh, meaning "it is because God has made me forget all my trouble and my father's household", and his second son Ephraim meaning "it is because God has made me fruitful in the land of my suffering". The names of both of these sons are a direct expression of Joseph's personal experience. God helped him to forget the pain of his past and the rejection of his brothers and in turn empowered him to prosper in a foreign land. His sons reflect his journey, both in history and destiny.[5]

Jabez is given his name by his mother and his name clearly reflects the pain of his birth. Jabez' name literally means "pain", potentially binding him the rest of his life to the pain of his mother.[6]

What is interesting in each of these examples is that the names did not reflect the experience of the person named, but rather of the person doing the naming. In each of these instances an experience, whether negative or positive, is imposed on someone else. Thus the implication is that the named person carries through life the aspirations or conclusions of someone else. The naming experience carries with it the possibility of entrapment or empowerment, depending on what it is.

It is important that we do not allow our lives to be defined or named by the experience of others. Think of it. How easy is it for parents to impose their angst or aspirations on their children? Or for leaders to burden their people? For us to create unrealistic and unkind expectations for the ones we love? Those of us who have the power to name, in other words who have significant influence over other people, must take care not to hurt or hinder those we love by projecting our experiences onto them, whether those experiences were good or bad. Sharing our wisdom is one thing, naming names is another.

If I can take this one step further. Don't allow any personal experience to define you. Life may have "happened" to you and whatever your role in the happening, you must remember that it only has the power to define or name you if you allow it. You may have failed, but you're not a failure. You may have been hurt, but you're not a victim. You may have experienced divorce, but without minimizing its seriousness we must remember that divorce is a "what" not a "who"! Things may have happened to us or because of us that we wish hadn't. We certainly need to take responsibility for these things and address them through God's truth. Having done this, however, we must move on from them and refuse them permission to take control of our destiny.

What experience has named and is defining you?

Named by purpose?

Two Joseph's, one in the Old Testament and the other in the New Testament, really help us with this. In Genesis 37 we're introduced to Joseph, son of Jacob, as the favoured son of his father, impacted by two profound dreams we assume come from God (although the text does not explicitly say). Thirteen years later, we see Joseph stand before Pharaoh helping to interpret the dreams which have so troubled the Egyptian ruler. Joseph not only gives them meaning, but out of that brings direction and, in doing so, earns himself a position as the second most powerful man in Egypt. Pharaoh gives Joseph the new Egyptian name of Zaphenath-Paneah, which means, "one who discovers hidden things".[7] This was the name Pharaoh gave to Joseph simply because this was what he saw in Joseph.

We meet our second Joseph in the book of Acts. He is actively involved in the early Church helping the poor, liquidizing assets to assist the Church and getting in among the people. Joseph so impressed and impacted the early Church community, that he was given a new name. He was called "Barnabas" which means "son of encouragement".[8] This was the name the Apostles gave to Joseph simply because this was what they saw in him.

Here we see two men named by the purpose and gifts they clearly expressed in their lives. The naming ceremony followed a life of action. These are cases of the name fitting the purpose. This begs an interesting question: if someone were to give us a name which reflected what they saw in us, what would our new name be? I know we may have designs on what we'd like it to be, because we think in our heads what we look like to others. But if we had no influence over the name people gave us other than the lifestyle they saw us consistently display, I wonder what they would call us? Is that a scary thought?

I suppose our hope would be that each of us would live so close to the purpose for which we believe we have been designed that there would be few choices left to the naming panel other than that which is obvious. The challenge to us, of course, is to live our lives in such an obvious way that the choice is a simple one.

Named by God?

When God gives us a name, He never makes a mistake. He not only has the power to name us, but any name He gives us will always reflect something of His glory and power. God-given names will always reflect our personhood, because He like no other knows who we are. The name He gives us points to our potential because He like no other knows what we have inside us. Our God-given name reflects our purpose because He like no other knows why we are here. I believe also that God delights to name us because He wants to lay claim to our lives. Any name given is forever associated with the one who gave it. God wants us to have a name, an identity that is forever linked to Him, so that when people look at us or are impacted by us, they think of Him.

Let me illustrate this through the names of two people God specially named. In both of these cases He refused to allow the powerful act of naming to be left to any human agent, instead He was the one who decided what both these men were called.

Zachariah should have named his son, but the chances are, had he done so, John (later called the Baptist) would not have been called John. Zachariah had no relatives called John and there was no historic reference for such a label. Therefore it would never have been in his thinking. That's why God took the naming responsibility off this man and took it up Himself. John means "grace or mercy of the Lord", and his name was to be a direct reflection of his distinctive purpose. John was not to live unto himself, but unto God. The gifts within John were to prepare for the specific task of being the harbinger for Jesus. For one so important and for a task so crucial, God was the One to give him his name.

"There came a man who was sent from God; his name was John."

(John 1:6)

Joseph didn't name Jesus, God did. Joseph was told to name Mary's firstborn by this specific name. Jesus means "Saviour or Deliverer", and this spoke clearly into the purpose for which He was born, "... *because he will save his people from their sins."*[9] The task for which Jesus was born was too important to leave His name to chance. He was named for the task. His personhood and purpose were linked from the very beginning through His God-given name. Jesus lived up to His name!

It's important that in order to discover our God-ordained identity we open our hearts to a God-given name. Our lives need to be aligned with God's intentions thus allowing God to "label" us out of His plan, thus delivering us from the prospect of being named or defined by the small things around us. We must let God set the agenda and determine our boundaries. We must invite the God who knows our name into the very centre of our world and allow Him to redefine that which He originally made. Our ambition must be to discover our God-given name, or put another way, our God-intended identity, and then with all our strength, live up to it!

What have you allowed to name or define you? Is it your history, your culture, your family, your pain or your dreams? Has God defined you or is someone or something else?

Names are important and it's vital we get the right one – His name!

> "...Before I was born the LORD called me;
> from my birth he has made mention of my name."
> (Isaiah 49:1)

Notes

1. Harry Rodger Webb is Cliff Richard. Brian Warner is Marilyn Manson. Paul David Hewson is Bono. Curtis James Jackson III is 50 Cent. Cheryl Sarkisian LaPierre is Cher. Diego de la Vega is Zorro. Edson Arantes do Nascimento is Pelé.
2. Rasputin, the Russian Monk.
3. Genesis 4:25–26.
4. Genesis 21:1–7.
5. Genesis 41:50–52.
6. 1 Chronicles 4:9–10.
7. Genesis 41:45.
8. Acts 4:36–37.
9. Matthew 1:21.

CHAPTER 6

Sale of the Century

Some would say that what happened on 1st December 1955 set in motion a chain of events that changed the United States of America forever. It was the day a young woman stood up by sitting down. Forty-two-year-old seamstress Rosa Louise McCauley Parks was returning home from work after a particularly tiring day. She waited for the bus to take her home, but the first one was completely full, offering no available seats, and so she decided to wait for the next one. Boarding the bus, she found an empty seat about half way down the bus, allowing her weary body a place to slump and rest. A few stops down the line a man boarded who angrily demanded Rosa's seat. The driver got involved and ordered Parks and three other passengers to vacate their seats or risk arrest. The other three moved, but Rosa Parks steadfastly refused and found herself arrested and taken to jail.

Rosa was a black woman in a white man's world. If she was to have any seat on the bus, it should have been at the back with all the other "blacks". However, the back of the bus was full and Rosa, as a black African American citizen of democratic America, took her seat and refused to give it up. On 6th December Parks was found guilty of a breach of city ordinance and charged $14.00. However, her simple act of defiance inspired many around her to begin boycotting the Montgomery bus company and for 381 consecutive days they did just that. Soon, the bus company was in financial ruin and racial segregation on buses was a thing of the past, confirmed in November 1956 when the Supreme Court, the highest court in America, ruled that segregation on buses was unconstitutional.[1]

Undoubtedly, the years of injustice she had witnessed and experienced produced a personal tipping point, causing her to stand up (or sit down, strictly speaking) and say "enough is enough". Looking back on this period of history it's hard to understand how any decent society could allow such practices to be endorsed and empowered by the law. Black Americans could fight and die for the Flag, but couldn't sit where they liked on a bus! I suspect, however, that although injustice played a big role in Rosa's decision, identity played an even greater one. Rosa Parks had a strong faith and commitment to the teachings of her church and somewhere, tucked in the pages of the Bible, is the teaching that humankind is made in the image of God ... *all humankind*. Rosa understood who she was. The law said she was a second-class citizen whose place was at the back of the bus, but she knew she was more than that and took the seat that she believed was rightly hers. One could argue it was only a seat, but for Rosa Parks this was a battle for identity and she was not prepared to give it up, regardless of the cost. The bus driver, James Blake, probably thought this was a fight over a seat, but for Mrs Rosa Parks this was a battle for her birthright!

Take a moment to read Genesis 25:27–34. If we wanted one story that represents the antithesis of Rosa Parks we wouldn't have to look much further than Esau. He was the firstborn son of his father Isaac, although it was a close run thing. He shared his mother's womb with his twin brother, Jacob. Even though Esau made it out first, as Jacob came out he was grasping his older brother's heel, hence his name, which literally means "he grasps the heel" and can by implication point to the idea of a deceiver! Being the first to pop out of his mother Rebekah, ensured Esau had firstborn status. This boy wasn't just born with a silver spoon in his mouth, he had a whole drawer full of golden ones! Esau didn't know it yet, but he had just hit the jackpot.

Being firstborn entitled Esau to a number of key things, but I want to draw your attention to just two.

Firstly, he would have authority and superiority over the rest of the family. After the passing of his father, Esau would have full authority over his father's estate. He would assume the role as family leader and the supreme place of honour that went with it. In fact, the head of the family became, in many respects, the priest of his home and estate. He would be responsible for the administration of spiritual leadership to those under his care. We see examples of this in Noah (Genesis 8:20), Abraham (Genesis 12:7), Isaac (Genesis 26:25), Jacob (Genesis 31:54) and Job (Job 1:5). It's not until the establishment of the Law that this responsibility is transferred from the firstborn to the tribe of Levi, whom God took *". . . in place of the first born male offspring of every Israelite woman"*.[2]

Secondly, he would inherit a double portion of his father's estate. The idea of a double portion for the firstborn son was later enshrined in the Law, guaranteeing protection of his rights as the firstborn.[3] However, Isaac, Esau and Jacob are pre-Law. It could be argued that the Law only allowed for a double portion to the firstborn to prevent other members of the family receiving no part of the inheritance at all. It suggests that a common pre-Law practice was that most, if not all, of the father's inheritance was given to the firstborn. This is clearly seen in the life of Abraham. Although he had other children to other wives (and gave some gifts to them), the Bible makes clear that Abraham *". . . left everything he owned to Isaac"*.[4]

Whichever way we look at it, Esau stood to inherit a fortune. Isaac's inheritance from his father made him wealthy and the Bible further shows that Isaac was shrewd by significantly increasing his wealth.[5] In short, Isaac was super-rich and Esau was either going to inherit a double portion of his father's super-rich estate or the whole lot!

It's important to know all this to help us grasp the immensity of the incredible statement uttered by Esau the firstborn:

> *"What good is the birthright to me?"*
>
> (Genesis 25:32)

The word "good" has been inserted in by the translators to help us grasp the significance of the statement. But even without it, it's still pretty shocking: *"What is the birthright to me?"*

However we read it, we're left wondering where Esau's head was at! Esau's "sale of the century" is rivalled only by the capitulation of his ancestors in the Garden of Eden. Let's do the maths. He's offering to sell his birthright and all it entails for a bowl of stew and some bread. Why on earth would Esau offer such a valuable item at such a bargain price? From the passage we conclude a number of possibilities.

He was hungry

> *"Quick, let me have some of that red stew! I'm famished."*
>
> (25:30)

Now there's hunger and there's hunger. Esau was a hunter and a man *". . . of the open country"*. I would suspect that because of this he was physically strong and accustomed to the sort of endurance needed to kill game with your bare hands and drag it home. So he's no weakling, yet he acts like one! There's no doubt he comes home hungry and his hunger pangs aren't helped by the fact his younger brother just happened to be cooking what might well have been one of Esau's favourite dishes. But Esau's reaction to the prospect of not getting some food is baffling:

"Look, I am about to die."

(25:32)

It seems that the first son of his father had become accustomed to the world of instant gratification. If he wanted something, he got it. Why should he have to wait for food, why couldn't he have it now? Facing the prospect of not getting what he wanted, when he wanted it, Esau overreacted. Esau looked like a man, he even had the muscles and scars to prove it, but it seems from this reaction, he was still a boy!

We need to learn the lesson well from Esau's antics. If we live a life based on the premise of instant gratification, of expecting always to get what we want, we are setting ourselves up not only for disappointment, but we are putting ourselves into a position of vulnerability and danger. A needy person will always be at the mercy of those who can supply. Esau "needed" food and Jacob just happened to have some. Suddenly, due to his lack of discipline and character, Esau's drawer full of golden spoons was about to be plundered for a price that borders on the criminal. If we live with this mentality, expecting and demanding things of God and of life, and behaving like children when we don't get what we want, when we want it, we open up the gates of our city to any invader whose offer is remotely attractive.

Get this: unrealistic demands often produce unfulfilled expectations which leads to unresolved disappointment which sets us up for unwise decisions.

He was exploited

Some would want to see Esau as the victim in all this. His scheming brother, born grasping the heel of his firstborn sibling, is just up to his old tricks. Jacob knows when Esau will return from the fields, he knows Esau's weaknesses, and he mercilessly exploits "his poor brother" to get what he's always wanted – the birthright! It's hard to conclusively argue this from the text, although one might want to site circumstantial evidence from the other events of Jacob's life, that this would fit the personality profile of the young man with the soft hands in the kitchen.

Did Jacob exploit Esau?

Only from the point of view that he offered a service at a price. The text clearly vindicates Jacob beyond this point. There is no coercion, no manipulation and certainly no force used. Jacob presents a business transaction and waits for Esau's response. Had Esau simply refused the offer, this story would never have made it into the pages of the Bible. Esau only had to say "no", to step back and see the big picture and, better still, call one of his many servants to fetch him the food he so desperately wanted. In a household this size, was Jacob the only cook or the only one cooking? The truth is, Jacob could only "take" from Esau that which his brother was prepared to give away!

Peter encourages us with these words:

> "*Be self-controlled and alert. Your enemy the devil prowls around like a roaring lion looking for someone to devour. Resist him, standing firm in the faith . . .*"

(1 Peter 5:8–9)

Though Peter presents us with a vivid description of the devil as a roaring lion (and if you've ever heard a lion roar, especially in the wild, you'll know how scary that can be), he also empowers us with the means to overcome such a foe. He tells us to do (therefore we can do) four things:

1. **Be self-controlled** – the word here means "to be sober", not to have our judgment clouded, but to be clear in our thinking.

2. **Be alert** – the word here points to vigilance, being aware of the enemy's movements and staying alert to the prospect of what is happening.

3. **Resist the devil** – the word here implies to be firm against an onslaught, to withstand. Though the onslaught may be severe, it can be resisted and conquered.

4. **Stand firm in our faith** – the word here suggests "to be solid in its place", by implication: having a strong foundation.

In short, Peter suggests that the devil can only take advantage of us, can only exploit us, if we let him! If we decide to resist, if we lay strong foundations and remain clear in our thinking, no bowl of stew will be able to take us from our convictions, no-matter how good it looks or how delicious it smells. Without this inner strength however, just like Esau, we're open to exploitation and we may find ourselves hearing our mouth say "yes", when really we know we ought to say "no"!

He was ignorant

It seems that the primary reason for this catastrophic decision is firmly located in Esau's lack of understanding of who he was and what he had. Esau was ignorant of the facts of his life. Had he truly understood who he was – the firstborn of his father's household – and had he grasped what he had – the privilege and empowerment of birthright – this deal would never have gone down. Jacob would have been shown the door and Esau would have remained the heir of his father, if a hungry one! Had Esau had the spirit, resolve and insight of Rosa Parks the story may well have ended very differently.

Perhaps you think I'm being too hard on the boy. I might agree with you if it wasn't for the words contained in the book of Hebrews:

"See that no one is sexually immoral, or is godless like Esau, who for a single meal sold his inheritance rights as the oldest son."

(Hebrews 12:16)

The Genesis account uncompromisingly states, *"So Esau despised his birthright"* (25:34). His actions seem to bear this out and the commentary of the writer to the Hebrews further confirms it. We are warned not to be "godless" like Esau. It is interesting that most commentators are careful to disassociate the first part of the verse, "sexually immoral", from Esau and suggest it is only the second part that applies to him, namely the godlessness. However, what is striking is that the word translated sexually immoral carries with it the imagery of selling – in this context, sexual selling or prostitution. Esau sold his birthright and although I would not want to stretch the point too far, the thought might remain, that in selling his birthright so cheaply, Esau prostituted the glory that was his. However, what cannot be disputed is that Esau's actions are seen as godless. In a moment of reckless ignorance he trampled underfoot that which was holy and treated a precious possession with scant regard.

What the writer of the Hebrews says next is startling:

"Afterward . . . when he wanted to inherit this blessing, he was rejected. He could bring about no change of mind, though he sought the blessing with tears."

(12:17)

As Esau tucked into his stew that day he had no idea of the cost of that meal, but one day he would. Despite his protestations, his tears and his repentance, his birthright was gone and he would never get it back. It truly was the sale of the century.

So what of you and me? What does Esau teach us in the twenty-first century? Take this one key truth from this chapter: if we don't know who we are in Christ and if we don't know what we've got in Christ, it leaves us vulnerable to the first attractive offer that comes along. We'll always settle cheaply if we're unsure of the value of that within our possession.

Rosa refused to give up her seat because she knew who she was and what she had. Esau virtually gave away a treasure because he was ignorant of his status. History marks them both, hailing one a hero and the other a fool. The same challenges they faced we encounter in one form or another almost every day. We must understand that the outcome of such events is not so much dependent on what is on offer, *but on what is within!*

Notes

1. http://www.gale.com/free_resources/bhm/bio/parks_r.htm – 7 May 2007.
2. Numbers 3:12–13; 8:14–18.
3. Deuteronomy 21:17.
4. Genesis 25:5.
5. See Genesis 26.

The Lost Boys

For my fortieth birthday, my wife Dawn bought me a portable satellite navigation system (sat nav) for my car. Even for the techno-challenged this is an invention of ingenious simplicity. Once powered and turned on, the little box requires only a postcode to get me to where I need to go. Within minutes I have a read out of the route, the mileage, and how long the journey will take. There's even a choice of voices to speak out the directions. I can have a choice of male or female, using either an English, American or Australian accent. I was disappointed there was no Irish accent! I mean, if the Aussies can get in, why can't the Irish? I can imagine it now. With *Danny Boy* playing softly in the background, a sweet Irish colleen whispers, "To be sure naow, you need to takin' the next rauight, that's if ya really want ta of caourse." (Knowing my luck I would end up with Betty from Belfast barking out instructions in some life-threatening way, "Right! Turn right naow, this instant ... or else!") Wouldn't it be good if we could choose whatever accent we wanted for our sat navs? What would you have and why? (Apart from Molly Malone whispering softly in my ear, I'd love to have a Birmingham accent: "Yam luvelaay!")

Apparently (and I know this is true because women have told

me), men are not good at asking for directions. The reasons range from being too proud to ask, to the fear of world war three breaking out in the car when the female navigator suggests, "You've missed the turn." Sometimes men optimistically believe that eventually it will work out, after all, there's bound to be a sign somewhere. And, of course, there are those stubborn few (I've never met any personally, you understand) who try to convince everyone in the car that they are not lost, just temporarily "out of position". Wasn't it Robert Frost who famously wrote, "Two roads diverged in a wood, and I took the one less travelled by, and that has made all the difference"?[1] Clearly another man in need of a sat nav for his birthday!

In Luke 15, Jesus is "provoked" into telling three powerful stories because of the attitudes of a group of religious onlookers, convinced that they were on the right road while everyone in the room, including Jesus Himself, was lost. Their sense of superiority permitted them to look down their self-righteous noses at every-one else and label them "sinners". Jesus tantalizes the crowd with the appetizing tales of the lost sheep and the lost coin before presenting the irresistible main dish of the story of "two" lost boys. As Jesus served it up to the eager gathering, this simple parable gave both delight and indigestion. In my Bible this final story carries the heading: "The Parable of the Lost Son", however, a closer examination of the story and the reason Jesus told it, shows us that actually there were two lost sons. The "lostness" of the younger is obvious. He gets his inheritance and leaves. But it is the lostness of the older son which is harder to discern. After all, he stays at home, remains with his father and is a good boy! I suggest to you that he was just as lost as his wandering brother and in fact that he is the focus of this story, not the pig-hugging prodigal!

There are few things more disturbing than meeting someone who is clearly lost when he is convinced he is not. In the crowd that day there were tax collectors and sinners, people who knew they were lost. Perhaps they were there looking for some direction from the teachings of Jesus. But mingling in the crowd were also those who were convinced they were on track when really they were just as lost as the "scum" they refused to mix with. Jesus' story of the two lost sons, one recklessly searching, the other stoically staying, spoke to everyone in the crowd. It offered divine navigation to destination freedom and true spiritual identity, but was anybody listening?

Jesus demonstrated the lostness of the lost sons in six crucial ways (three each). Through each lesson, Jesus the Way attempts to signpost His listeners, all of us, in the right direction. (I hope as the reader you understand, that when I use the term "son" or "boy" in this context, I am referring to the story, but the lessons I seek to draw are generic, applicable to both men and women.)

For a lost son – waiting is not an option

"Father, give me my share of the estate."

(v. 12)

Even the most patient among us wrestles with impatience. We all fall into the temptation of wanting what we want, right now! As one wag put it, "I think I'm a very patient person, until I'm asked to wait." Impatience is not a sign that we have lost our identity or are confused about who we are, it just means we're human. However, in this context it goes beyond impatience. This story illustrates a lack of trust in the processes of normal growth and life. For the person lost within, their lack of rest in their own personhood often manifests in their frustration with the ordinary, the routine and the mundane. If nothing looks like it is happening they try to make something happen and if that doesn't work they either don't accept it or try to force a change.

The younger son wanted his inheritance *now*. He believed that getting it now would help him discover life in a more fulfilling and enjoyable way. Tragically, all it really did was make him a "rich" lost boy, for he was lost before he left home. Though he lived in a new place, with new friends and newfound wealth, he was still lost! We must not be fooled into thinking that getting what we want (or think we want) will bring meaning or identity to our lives. Moving the furniture, increasing the bank balance or changing our environment isn't necessarily the answer to discovering who we are. Society has sold us the lie that this is so and many have bought the ticket only to discover they are still strangers in their own body.

When we know who we are, waiting becomes a little easier for the following reasons:

Firstly, we understand that our wealth resides not only in what we will get, but in what we already have. Secondly, we accept that if there is more to get, it will come through the wise management of what we already have. Thirdly, we rest in the satisfaction that even if there is no more, we have lived well and honoured God with all He has given to us.

Perhaps it is time that as blessed sons of our Father, we stopped asking for more and started recognizing, celebrating and utilizing what we have!

For a lost son – the answer is always "out there"

> *"Not long after that, the younger son got together all he had, set off for a distant country . . ."*

> (v. 13)

Jesus made it clear that the young man wanted to get as far away as possible from his father and the constraints of home by travelling to a "distant country". Far off fields have a tendency to look greener when we believe they hold some answers. The green field of course can be almost anything. I've seen "green field" syndrome kick in when it comes to churches, partners, jobs and even cars! The ignorance of this lost son was such that he couldn't see what was right in front of him, while at the same time being convinced that somewhere "out there" was the answer to all his desires and aspirations. Of course, there's nothing wrong with casting our vision over the horizon beyond the limitation of our current experience, this is a natural thing to do. But, we must not allow our vision of far off fields to be fuelled by a distorted understanding of where we are and what we have, or by some naïve assumption that somehow life "out there" will be different or better than life here. We must remember that wherever we go, *we are there* and unless something is changing inside us we are simply transporting our lostness to another place. On the surface a lot has changed, but in reality life is just the same! The green field of "out there" will only materialise when we make a journey of growth and development as people, living in the power of truth and in the revelation of who we really are. We must always remind ourselves that biblical pilgrimage places more emphasis on personhood than places. God is less concerned with where we are, than with who we are where we are! The tragedy is that many people, like our first lost son, find themselves in the wrong place because they never truly addressed the lostness within their being in the first place. They believe that the answer can be found "out there" when it lies "in here" – through a the heart tuned into their Creator.

For a lost son – security resides in earned status

> *"Father, I have sinned against heaven and against you. I am no longer worthy to be called your son."*

(v. 21)

If you've read the story you know that the son who left home fell on hard times, came to his senses and decided to return home. However, what is really interesting is the language Jesus puts in the boy's mouth. He uses two powerful words:

" ... I have **sinned** ... " (emphasis added). The word here points to the idea of missing the mark.

" ... I am no longer **worthy** ... " (emphasis added). The word here suggests the idea of deserving or of "earning" a reward.

Some would want to argue that in one sense this is a good thing. The young man had gone off, blown his money on wine, women and song and returned empty handed. He had sinned against both God and his father, and it is only fitting that he showed some serious repentance for what he had done. I'm all for true repentance. However, I suggest from the context that this was not the only motivation for this language. Earlier in the story when the young man is debating his predicament with himself, he is convinced that his place as a son has been lost and that the only option open to his father is to make him one of his "hired men". Could it be that his talk of unworthiness was less to do with sin and more to do with status? In his own words, he had missed the mark and was undeserving of any kindness or position within the home of his birth. If we flipped the story on its head and the son had returned rich, famous and honoured, he would never have considered his status as a son under threat, yet now he does. Why? His security as a son did not reside in who he was, the son of his father, but in what he did. So, when he returned as a loser (though still a son), he was convinced that the only status his actions merited was that of a paid employee.

When our value system is driven by a mentality of earned status the understanding of our identity will be more associated with works (what we do) than with grace (what He has done). There are sons reading these words who feel "more like a son" when they do well. Conversely, they feel like a hired employee the worse they do. I in no way wish to minimise the seriousness of sin, for God hates it. But neither do I want to go easy on graceless sonship for I believe this offends God just as grievously. John makes it clear that when we believe, we are given the right, the authority, to be called children of God (John 1:12), a status given to us through grace by our heavenly Father. Yet how it must upset Him when His children try to live in the purgatory of earned status instead of the freedom of grace-empowered sonship.

Let me ask you a question. Think about this seriously. When the son returned that day to the father, what would have offended the father more? A dishevelled, smelly, bankrupted son, or the suggestion that his son was no longer worthy to be his son and fit only to live with the servants? Sonship cannot be earned, only conferred. Sonship is a gift of grace and the proof that we are not lost boys is that we understand this and from this position of truth make it our ambition to please the Father, not in an attempt to earn His favour but to celebrate it!

For a lost son – it's hard to celebrate others

"The older brother became angry and refused to go in."

(v. 28)

The older brother found it impossible to celebrate with his father or for his brother. He could not celebrate because he was angry. As one commentator suggests, this was not "... a mere temporary fit of passion, but ... a deep seated wrath".[2] Perhaps resentment had built up in the heart of the older brother while the younger was away doing his thing. Therefore, when the wanderer returned, his brother exploded in disgust! It's hard to celebrate with someone else when anger dominates the heart.

Why was he so angry? The Bible doesn't say and I must be careful not to read too much in the Scriptures, but from the context I'll hazard this guess. Could it be that his anger was motivated not so much by the riotous living of his brother (although that's clearly the target), but by the discontent within his own heart, far from his own dreams and the life he wanted to live? It's interesting that Judas (a thief) became indignant at the "waste" of a woman's lavish gift of worship.[3] It's striking that King David ordered the execution of a "lamb stealing" citizen when he had stolen another man's wife and the life of one of his mighty men.[4] The issue at the root of their own dysfunction became the whip with which they judged and criticised others. Could it be that the anger of the older son was as much about himself as it was about his brother? Whatever the reason, he could not celebrate. The scene of the older brother, pouting like a child outside the party, revealed as much about his own lostness as the apparent condition of his newly found brother.

People who struggle with personal identity will always find it difficult, if not impossible, to celebrate the successes and achievements of others. I have been in full-time church leadership since 1987 and in those years it has been rare to find leaders who truly celebrate the success of another leader, church or ministry. Petty jealousy, mean-mindedness and snide comments say more about the condition of the speaker than the one being spoken of. Such behaviour reveals, at its core, a person not at rest with themselves. For lost boys, the success of others is a signal for only one kind of party – a pity-party!

If you know who you are it will empower you to celebrate with and for others and their success will never threaten you!

For a lost son – superiority masks insecurity

"But when this son of yours who has squandered your property with prostitutes comes home, you kill the fattened calf for him!"

(v. 30)

The older brother's superiority is expressed in the most brutal fashion by Jesus. He refers to his brother as *"this son of yours"*, making an assumption that his brother wasted his wealth (though he refers to it as his father's) on prostitutes. His self-righteousness cannot be disguised – a message not lost on the "morally superior" religious types in the crowd, whose disingenuous comments provoked the three-part mini-series in the first place.

When we are insecure we thrive on putting others down, exposing their inferiority while actually highlighting our own superiority. This is a blunt and ineffective tool that may have some short-term instant gratification, but will ultimately produce absolutely nothing of substance and life. It does not require any moral fibre or intelligence to put another person down for the enhancement of personal ego. However, as attractive as the put down may seem at the time, it reveals an ugliness of heart and a bitterness of spirit which will ultimately maroon us on the island of our own making . . . superior, but all alone!

People secure in their identity and personhood do not need badges, places of honour or a personal assistant constantly reminding them of their greatness. They don't need to live in the world of the put down, or of doing unto others but doing it first! They have no interest in expressing their superiority over others for they know this is a hollow and futile pursuit that not only hurts those around them, but also themselves. "This son of yours . . ." was his brother, yet the older brother regarded his own flesh and blood with disdain and scant regard. Though the actual words aren't spoken, they echo through every syllable: "I'm better than him!"

As you read these words, I urge you not to live in such a dark world. The apparent inferiority of others is no comfort to you if you are lost too. Smug superiority breeds in a heart that has forgotten who it is and why they have what they have. Looking down your nose at others is not a sign of greatness, but weakness.

Putting others down doesn't make you look good, rather it's ugly and unbecoming of any son of the Father. Always remember, you are what you are and you have what you have because of the lavish generosity of your heavenly Father.[5] When you're tempted to lord it over others, this truth will keep your feet firmly on solid, life-changing ground.

For a lost son – a slave resides within

"Look! All these years I've been slaving for you and never disobeyed your orders. Yet you never gave me even a young goat so I could celebrate with my friends."

(v. 29)

In the same way that the language of the youngest son gave away the condition of his heart when he returned to his father, so it is with the older brother. Again the words placed in his mouth by the Master reveal something of the intent of Jesus to communicate with certain sections of the crowd. Look at how the oldest son describes his relationship with his father:

*"All these years I've been **slaving** for you and never **disobeyed your orders.**"*

(emphasis added)

On the surface he had remained a dutiful and helpful son, but these words, expressed in the pressure of the moment, revealed the heart of a slave beating within him. He saw his service as duty to orders and his responsibility as slavish obedience. Though he too had received his inheritance from his father he still believed he was impoverished. I wonder how shocked and offended the father would have been to hear such sentiments?

Is it possible to be a son and think and live like a slave?

Tragically, I know this to be true, for I have done it. Too often I have approached the throne of grace like a nervous intruder. When asked to take my place at the banquet table heavy with good gifts, I've frowned at my name card and wondered if there was another John Andrews in the building. When offered gifts of generosity from my Father, instead of receiving them with thanks as He expects, I've worked a little bit harder to justify to myself my worthiness for the gift. Now I know you've never done anything like that ... but just in case you have, you need to face up to the truth that such a mentality is slave thinking and that sons must not think like this!

Strangely, when it comes to our heavenly Father, there is that within us that finds some "comfort" in the doing of a slave than in the privileges of a son. At times it doesn't "feel" quite right, so we do something just to make us "feel better". Though our Father is patient with us as we make our journey, He passionately hates the slave mentality that tries to usurp authority within us. He wants us to come to the table as sons and live like we belong.

When I got married, I was not only blessed with an amazing wife, but Fiver the border collie dog came as part of the package – "have dog will travel". Fiver (don't ask) was a beautiful, gentle and intelligent hound, loved by everyone who met her. One day, as I was munching on a little breakfast, I noticed her sitting in front of me staring intently at the morsels disappearing into my mouth. I couldn't resist those gorgeous eyes, so I threw her a scrap that vanished in double quick time. As she devoured the offering, God spoke to me in an unmistakable, life-changing way. He said, "Crumbs are for dogs, not for children." What a life-changing revelation that became for me, literally setting me on a journey of transformation. As a son, wrestling with the slave within, I had settled so often for crumbs, but that day I became convinced that God had much more for me. I've tried to live like a son ever since! Why not join me?

The answer for both sons was in the truth of the father's statement,

"My son ... everything I have is yours."

(v. 31)

In this statement we observe the position and privilege of sonship. Both of these boys needed to remind themselves of who they were – *sons* – and of what they had – *everything the father possessed*. The lost boys did not know who they were or what they had. As a result one left home, squandered his wealth and came to impoverishment, while the other stayed at home, hoarded his wealth and settled for impoverishment. Jesus doesn't give us an end to the story, rather it finishes with the touching plea of the father. Perhaps the Master deliberately left the story open-ended and by doing so invited His audience to decide on their own ending.

That's the power we have today, for our story isn't finished yet. The decisions we make today will determine whether we live as lost boys or sons of the Father. Make a choice today not to be a lost boy, but to be a son. The Father is waiting and everything He has is yours!

Notes

1. From his poem, *The Road Not Taken*. No desecration of a great poem intended.
2. Vincent's New Testament Word studies.
3. Mark 14:1–11.
4. 2 Samuel 12:1–10.
5. James 1:17–18.

Heaven's Eyes

Guess who? Inspired by the motto "Aim high even if you hit a cabbage", given to her by her grandfather Dubby Jones, she's certainly hit a little higher than that. She has represented her country at the highest sporting level and achieved virtually everything within her field. Over the course of her career she has won a total of sixteen Olympic medals, including eleven golds, held over thirty world records in events including 100m, 200m, 400m, 800m, 1,500m, 5,000m, 10,000m, 10km road and half marathon, and won the London Marathon six times between 1997 and 2002 (are you tired yet?).

Her name is Tanni Grey-Thompson and what's remarkable about all her sporting achievements is that they've all been accomplished while sitting in a wheelchair. At 1.25 am on 26th July, 1969, Tanni was born at Glossop Terrace Hospital in Cardiff ... with spina bifida. Many would have viewed this as an insurmountable challenge, condemning her to a life of limitation. Any idea of sporting ambition was out of the question, surely? However, it seems Tanni had different ideas. She saw herself and her world through different eyes and that seems to have made all the difference.

Tanni says, "I've never thought why me? I've never cried

because I'm in a wheelchair and I've never felt bitter. This is just the way it is. People feel sorry for me and assume I've got a sad, tragic life because they don't look past the chair. But if it doesn't bother me, why should it bother anyone else? ... 'I've got it, there's nothing I can do about it, so I might as well get on with it.' That's always been my attitude." [1]

Sometimes when we talk like this and use such examples as Tanni Grey-Thompson, Christians become nervous, fearing a humanist agenda, mind-over-matter philosophy, or a doctrine that drifts towards self-reliance rather than divine assistance. I understand this concern. We must learn to walk a pilgrimage that balances the utter necessity of the Divine in our lives, His Word, His power and His presence, without which we are truly lost, with our responsibility to engage our minds, bodies and lifestyles in such a way that "assists" God to do in us that which He has always desired to do. Our mind, our confessions and our choices have the power to limit God's influence in our lives and can trap us in a prison of limitation for which we were never designed. How we see ourselves is one such factor. If we cannot "see beyond the chair", if we fail to see the divine design that marks us or what heaven sees when it looks at us, we will always struggle to believe in a God who believes in us!

> "... do not think of yourself more highly than you ought, but rather think of yourself with sober judgment, in accordance with the measure of faith God has given you."
>
> (Romans 12:3)

The phrase "sober judgment" comes from a word which means "to be of sound mind, to think discreetly, soberly and wisely". It is interesting that when interpreting the phrase we tend to speak of not thinking too highly of ourselves. This of course is clear and understandable from the context used by Paul, but the word itself urges us to have a proper estimation of ourselves. So, although the immediate context encourages us not to have an "inflated" view of who we are, is it too much to suggest that the word may also encourage us not to have a "deflated" view of ourselves?

Over the years of my journey I have met relatively few people I would have deemed truly arrogant, with an inflated sense of self-worth or importance. In my experience, the vast majority of those I have encountered have struggled with a seriously deflated view of themselves, with a self-image that is less than they truly are. The lion's share of my energy as a leader has been expended in trying to build people up to something that reasonably resembles heaven's view. I'm not saying arrogance or egotism are not issues in life of the Church, because they are. There are those who see themselves through pride-tinted lenses, allowing rampant ego-inflation to hurt themselves and those around them. Without doubt, over-evaluation of self is unacceptable to God, but so, I would suggest, is under-evaluation. When a man or woman declares themselves to be useless, worthless and a waste of space, though I understand where such angst may come from, it is nonetheless an evaluation which is off the mark and, dare I say it, entirely offensive to God our maker, the One who does all things well! My desire is that you would be challenged to have a sober judgment of yourself. Not too high, but not too low; that you would learn to see yourself as you really are, through heaven's eyes.

Some have argued that self-image is driven by what we believe people think about us. The influence of family, friends, enemies, community and society at large can have a huge bearing on how any individual sees themselves in terms of beauty, worth or purpose. The Bible, however, encourages us to move the focus of such evaluation away from the people around us to the God who loves us. Does this seem glib and impossible? If it's true that the opinions of others have helped shape and form our estimation of ourselves, then is it also possible for God's opinion of us to inspire a new understanding of how we see ourselves?

There's a story in the Bible which illustrates this clash of vision perfectly. It's found in Judges 6:11–24, although it might be worthwhile reading the whole chapter to set it in context. We pick up the story with a young man called Gideon who is threshing wheat in a winepress. His land is under brutal occupation and this clandestine act is the only way he knows of keeping his precious harvest from the clutches of his enemy. The angel of the Lord appears to him and a conversation ensues on a subject on which Gideon and the divine messenger have two diametrically opposing views. When it comes to who Gideon is, what he sees and what heaven sees could not be further apart.

In this encounter what comes to the surface is what Gideon truly thinks of himself, provoked to some degree by what God says of him. He is open and honest with his visitor and what he says gives us a clue as to why he was where he was, threshing wheat in a winepress.

Heaven's eyes

"The LORD is with you, mighty warrior."

(v. 12)

The Lord hits Gideon with a double whammy. Contained within this seemingly simple statement are two potential life-changing truths for the young wheat-thresher. There is an assurance that God is with him and that he, that's right, the bloke hiding in the winepress for fear of his enemies, is in fact a mighty warrior! This was how God saw Gideon. No one else looking on that day would have dared venture such a conclusion about a man in such inauspicious surroundings, clutching his meagre bounty. But this is what God saw and He declared it unerringly to Gideon.

Gideon's eyes

> "... *if the* LORD *is with us, why has all this happened to us? ... But now the* LORD *has abandoned us and put us into the hand of Midian.*"
>
> (v. 13)

Gideon's response completely ignores God's estimation of him that he is a mighty warrior. Instead, he zeroes in on the first part, revealing his own theological position. His theology was warped on at least two counts. Firstly, at no time had God abandoned him or his people, in fact they were the ones that had abandoned God. (It's interesting how time has the effect of changing the facts of history.) Secondly, his conclusion that God had left the building made it possible for him to miss what was right in front of him. Even if we want to argue that the angel standing in front of him wasn't the Lord Himself, at the very least it was His representative. Ironic, isn't it, debating God's absence when He's in the room! That's the power of our theology or our understanding (or lack of it) of God. This will directly impact how we view our world and ourselves. With God gone, Gideon saw his world as hopeless and his boundaries as narrow. The tragedy was that he was convinced of his own take on the truth instead of embracing the truth now being revealed to him.

Heaven's eyes

> "*Go in the strength you have and save Israel out of Midian's hand.*"
>
> (v. 14)

God's response to Gideon's warped conclusions is not to engage in an argument, but to press on with His intention to transform the wheat-thresher into a willing warrior. The Lord now turns His attention from how Gideon should view Him, to how Gideon should see himself. Because Gideon apparently ignored God's insistence that he was a mighty warrior, the Lord decided to drive the point home. Note again that God's estimation and evaluation of this young man is in the present, not the future. God urges Gideon to go in the strength he has – not will have or might have, but has right now! It seems Gideon already had the strength within him to save his nation, but something was preventing it from being released. He didn't need to go away to warrior school, climb a mountain and meditate, or pray and fast, he just had to acknowledge what Almighty God had already put within him and let it out! It goes back to the idea of being pre-packed. Everything God was ever going to ask Gideon to do, He had already equipped him for. Heaven could see it . . . but could he?

Gideon's eyes

"*. . . how can I save Israel? My clan is the weakest in Manasseh, and I am the least in my family.*"

(v. 15)

Hold it, before we proceed, let's set the atmosphere. Perhaps a lone violinist playing something mournful and melancholic, lower the lights and get the tissues out. Here it comes! It seems God has got it wrong again. Apparently He does that a lot . . . turns up at the wrong address, a case of mistaken identity. "God, You've got the wrong man, You must mean someone else!" If God's evaluation of Gideon is that he's a strength-filled mighty warrior, clearly Gideon had missed that seminar. His estimation is one of smallness, weakness and ineffectiveness. "I can't because I'm small, I can't because we're weak – I can't because . . . I can't!"

Do you see the challenge God has? His hardest task is not defeating the Midianites but convincing one of His own sons that indeed he is a son, that he has the strength and that he can do what he is being asked to do. Gideon was in the winepress because the winepress was in him. He was comfortable in such a small place because his personal theology excused it and his own self-evaluation permitted it. If God has left and Gideon is only one step up the pecking order from a worm, a winepress could be justified as a pretty adventurous place. But for a warrior, it's a coffin! If God was to get Gideon out of the winepress He had to get the winepress out of Gideon. The only answer to this dilemma was a transformed theology and a renewed personality.

Heaven's eyes – the final word

> *"I will be with you and you will strike down all the Midianites together."*
>
> (v. 16)

Gideon's had his say and now heaven has the final word. The Lord speaks again and in essence repeats what He has already said – only necessary when we're not getting it. Gideon is assured again of the presence of God and of his own importance and influence as a man. The Almighty is not hyping the young man up into a testosterone-filled frenzy, rather He is once again confronting him with the facts, the truth of His God and of himself. This and only this will empower Gideon beyond the boundaries of winepress-ville into the purpose for which he was born.

Going back to Paul's words about viewing ourselves with sober judgment, was this the case for Gideon? Perhaps we may want to argue that this story demonstrates God's power to lift the humble to new levels. However, could it be that this is a story about God lifting the deflated to a normal or expected level? Could it be that Gideon, like so many, was living below the basic line of God's expectation for him because he had accepted a view of himself (and his God) which was so debilitating that it prevented him from impacting the world he was called to save? There was no danger of having an inflated ego, he was full of himself alright . . . but surely the wrong self! The self in the winepress was not the self God had made and was one the Almighty was not prepared to put up with.

Some years ago I was invited to speak to a group of leaders on the subject of "building bigger people". A few days after my engagement, I received a letter from a leader who had been present. The contents (all four A4 pages), were filled with anger and disgust that I could preach such heresy, designed only to lead the faithful astray from the Word of God. "God does not want bigger people, He wants smaller people who know they are nothing, unworthy and valueless without Him." He was concerned that bigger people would rely on themselves and no longer look to God. Of course, there's always a danger of moving away from God whatever our size, but somehow we don't seem to notice a similar lack of reliance on God when it is cloaked in the language of apparent humility and self-effacement. Pride and arrogance are always lurking dangers, but so is thinking that moves beyond humility or sober judgment into self-loathing or a lack of self-respect. When I look through the Bible I see God building bigger people everywhere. Abram became Abraham, Jacob became Israel, a shepherd became a king, and a bunch of northern teenagers became the pillars of the Church. The old Pentecostals called it "redemption and lift", the power of the good news to transform lives. I would suggest to you if you're not a bigger person after meeting Jesus than you were before, something's not right!

When Michael Gill was about to finish sixth grade his teacher, Miss Markham, invited him to her home for tea. She took out a note and showed it to him. It was written in large, bold handwriting and she asked him to read what she had written. Nervously, he read the words, *"Michael Gates Gill is destined to be great"*. As he looked at his teacher thinking that perhaps there was more to read, she smiled, took him by the hand and spoke to him. "I have made a decision . . . you Michael are destined for *greatness*. I don't care what you do, or what you don't do. I don't care if you go to some prestigious college, or don't go. I just know: You *are* great." Years later Michael met Miss Markham again, having just returned from Yale University, sure that she would be proud of his achievement. Undoubtedly she was, but her parting comment to him was a reminder of what she saw: "It's not what you do, it's who you are. And you are great."[2]

Reading this story it's clear that Miss Markham saw something that Michael Gates Gill didn't see. She looked into the heart of a young man and saw not only his potential but his personhood. Even for one so young, she was willing to go out on a limb and confess what she believed and what she saw. Isn't that just like our relationship with God? Isn't that what we see take place in the winepress? Just as Miss Markham tried to convince her young pupil of what she saw in him, so God tries to convince us of what He sees in us. If we can see what He sees then everything will change!

I love what Brennan Manning says in this context from his book, *The Relentless Tenderness of Jesus*. "Take sides with God against your own self-evaluation." How easy and natural it is for us to trust our own opinions, however they have been shaped by those around us. How difficult it is to believe the word of another, when it flies in the face of that of which we have become convinced. It requires courage to believe what God says about us when His words challenge us to leave the comfort of our winepress and engage with a world of opportunities. Believing God's estimation about us will bring change within which will be expressed in change without. Seeing ourselves through heaven's eyes means we cannot stay the same and our present boundaries will not be able to contain the self we become – the self that God made us to be.

My granny used to say, "What you don't know won't hurt you." However, in this context nothing could be further from the truth. What Gideon didn't know *was* hurting him. His misunderstanding of God's role in his life and the warped evaluation of his own personhood meant that he was missing the best for his life and was living well within the borders of restriction, and that's got to hurt! If we fail to grasp who God is and who we are, this will inevitably hurt us. Not knowing these truths will ensure we do not live the life we were purposed to and that the person we are will be a pale imitation of the person we are supposed to be. If we come to understand that the Lord is with us, that we are in fact much more than we think we are, then we can impact and change our world.

Tanni Grey-Thompson looked beyond her wheelchair and surprised the world. Gideon looked beyond the winepress and saved his world. In his case, a little knowledge, at least of the right things, was a good thing. Empowered by heaven's vision of him, he left the winepress and impacted his world. I wonder what might happen to our world if we dare to see ourselves through heaven's eyes?

Notes _____

1. Grey-Thompson, T., *Seize the Day, The story of a heroine of our time*, Hodder & Stoughton, 2001, pp. xi–xv, 1–2 & 228.
2. Gill, M.G., *How Starbucks Saved My Life*, HarperCollins, 2007, pp. 62–65.

When You're Not You

From a Christian perspective, if there was one person whom we could assume had no confusion surrounding His own identity then surely it would be Jesus. The Gospels are more than clear as to His identity and none of them even hint at the prospect that Jesus was nothing less than sure about who He was and what He was on the earth to do. However, what is interesting are some comments made by Dr Luke as he sought to make the identity of Jesus clear to current and potential followers.

> *"...the Holy Spirit descended on him [Jesus] in bodily form like a dove. And a voice came from heaven: 'You are my Son, whom I love; with you I am well pleased.'"*
>
> (Luke 3:22)

That's great – crystal clear! Luke then follows the statement from heaven with a comment of his own: *"Now Jesus himself was about thirty years old when he began his ministry. He was the son, **so it was thought**, of Joseph, the son of Heli..."* (Luke 3:23).[1]

Luke goes on in the same chapter to make it clear that Jesus' genealogy extends all the way back to God and in Luke's writings, both his Gospel and the book of Acts, there is no doubt that he believed Jesus was the Son of God in flesh, come to save the world. What is fascinating, however, is that within the space of a few sentences two potentially very different views of Jesus are presented. One voice, the Father, speaks from heaven and affirms Him as His Son, deity in flesh; the other, the perception or opinions of society, that He was, *"so it was thought"* the son of Joseph, that is, an ordinary man. There is, of course, no hint on Luke's part that there was any confusion in the mind of Jesus, but the implication is that his readers might not be so certain. It is interesting that when Jesus leaves the Jordan and goes into the wilderness, a battle rages over truth which has at its core the identity of Jesus: *"If You are the Son of God..."* (emphasis added).

Followers and opponents have debated the identity of Jesus for over 2,000 years and it seems that every generation since His death and resurrection has been scandalized by the paradox of His identity. Baffled by the glory of the incarnation, finite human minds have struggled to grasp the magnitude of the infinite and the apparent contradiction of God in human form. Even today many look at Jesus yet don't recognise Him, while others look and see His glory.[2] The identity of Jesus continues to challenge us not only intellectually, but spiritually. If such a thing were possible, that God could become one of us, what does that teach us about God and what does it tell us about humanity?

Pages have been and will be filled with words greater than mine on this awesome subject and it's tempting to stay here, but I want us to consider for a moment the journey that Jesus Himself made in understanding who He was and what He had come to do. As we've already seen, the Bible teaches that our identity is linked to our destiny. Who we are is linked to what we are here to do. Confusion on one will inevitably lead to pollution of the other. They are two inseparable halves of the same whole.

Jesus had to contend with a singular identity touched by two very different worlds, as captured so succinctly by Luke's account. Jesus heard His Father proclaim *"You are my Son"*, yet He had a human mother and carried her family's physical similarities, shaped by centuries of genetic development. The culturally tainted images of religious painters who have presented Jesus as having blonde hair, blue eyes and white skin are understandable in the context of their day, but nonetheless preposterous. Jesus looked like everyone else around Him and yet was uniquely different from every human being on the planet at that time. He learned to live with the paradox of being the son of a woman and the Son of God all at the same time. If there was one person entitled to have some identity issues, it was Jesus.

In order for Jesus to become the Saviour of the world it was crucial He not only understood who He was, but was able to handle such an identity. His destiny demanded the fusion of deity and humanity and a life lived in submission to that identity and purpose. As God He had to learn to live under the constraint of human limitation and as a man He had to learn how to handle the glory of being the Creator and Sustainer of the universe without letting the secret out. Those who lived with Him in Nazareth were permitted only to see His ordinariness until the time was right to be more open with His purpose. Jesus did such a good job of holding these dynamics in tension that even when He performed miracles in His home town, most stumbled over His claims because they couldn't see past the fact that He was Mary's son – a simple home town carpenter![3] Is it any wonder Mary hid so much in her heart? Even now, after two millennia of post-Jesus history and trillions of words written on this mesmerizing man, my mind still spins in wonder.

At the age of twelve He knew He was the Son of His Father and had an insight into what His purpose was.[4] By thirty He stood in a synagogue, empowered by the Holy Spirit, confidently announcing the "year" of God's jubilee and favour to the world.[5] Seven times He was able to confidently proclaim "I AM",[6] revealing that His food was to do the will of the One who sent Him.[7] The Bible is silent about those first thirty years of Jesus' life (with the exception of His temple excursion), however we are told that Jesus grew in wisdom (intellectually), stature (physically), in favour with God (spiritually) and men (emotionally/relationally)[8] and that He learned to walk obediently through the things He suffered.[9] By the time Jesus left the carpenter's shop and hit the planet He had a clear understanding of His identity and, because of this, His destiny and in that our eternal hope was secure. Jesus lived as the person He was meant to be and because of this we have the possibility of experiencing divine life and purpose. Jesus demonstrates to us the power of life lived out of the empowerment of its original design. His life is an example to us all of the need to discover our God-ordained identity which then releases us into a destiny of fulfilment, meaning and purpose. The clarity with which Jesus understood His identity saved Him from some serious consequences.

Mistaken identity

When I was a child I remember watching the 1956 B-movie version of *The Body Snatchers*. It terrified me then as I watched it on our black and white TV (not only were our pictures in black and white, but there was no remote control. Can you imagine it, having to actually walk across the room to change channels? I'm not sure my children could cope with such a reality). I've seen the film as an adult and I laughed at the bits that really scared me. Now it seems so wooden, out-of-date and obvious, but back then it was behind the settee stuff. The plot revolves around the fact that people are being replaced by alien copies grown from plant like pods who kill their human victims. The replacements are identical in every way except that they are devoid of all emotion. The aliens never seemed to blink, they walked slowly everywhere (but always seemed to catch their victim) and talked in heavily accented speech: "Hel . . . lo. My . . . name . . . is . . . " No one in the town seemed to notice this strange behaviour. Maybe that's why the aliens landed there! Getting back to the point, the aliens were impostors, impersonating the person whose life they had now stolen. However, no matter how perfect the physical copy, the real person was gone.

Is it possible to be an impostor in our own body? If we are not careful we become expert at pretending and comfortable with a lifestyle of hypocrisy – not moral hypocrisy in this context (good on the outside, bad on the inside), but identity hypocrisy, denying who we are, determined to wear any mask that fits. The problem with wearing masks is that we've got to remember which one we wore the last time we were there. It becomes a taxing and demotivating pursuit, driven by the need to escape ourselves or please other people. Liberation from maskville, from the grasp of those body snatchers, enables us to become secure in our own personhood and celebrate the fit of our own skin.

When Judas led the mob to arrest Jesus, they were asked who they were looking for. They answered, "Jesus of Nazareth." Jesus replied to them (three times) *"I am he!"*[10] There were many views of who Jesus was. He was variously seen as the carpenter, Mary's son, an agent of Satan, a political threat, a good teacher from God, the reincarnation of one of the prophets, a friend of sinners, the son of David, a drunk and a glutton, a heretic and blasphemer! However, Jesus knew exactly who He was. The opinions of family, friends and enemies didn't impact Him because He was secure in His own skin. He was able to stand before a crowd and express exactly who He was. In the dark, misty garden there was no chance of mistaken identity!

Misplaced energy

Working hard is good, but working smart is even better. I was raised in a household committed to a strong work ethic that I've gladly bought into. I love work and enjoy the feeling of having given my best in a situation or project. But I've discovered it is even more fulfilling when my energy output is expended on something that I believe in, that reflects my purpose and that contributes to that for which I was made.

After a particularly long day, I returned home at about 9.15 pm to be greeted by the small group being hosted in our home. As I sat down with my friends enjoying a much needed cup of coffee, I was asked if I was tired. In truth I was, yet as I thought about the question, I realised that I'd been engaged that day in things that years before I had dreamed of doing. Quite literally I was living my dream and understood that this was one of the major factors (not the only one) for my high levels of energy. I suppose that had I just returned home after a twelve-hour shift from a job I hated, with no sense of big-picture destiny attached to my endeavour, I may have responded to the question differently. Most nights I go to bed tired, but fulfilled!

Where are you putting your energy? Is it going into the people and things you love and the areas you believe in? Does it reflect what you believe is the purpose of your life? Is the job really an expression of you or a means to an end? Are you living your dream? So often when I've challenged people with these questions they've reacted with phrases like "Beggars can't be choosers" or "It's okay for you!" Though I fully understand this reaction, it makes assumptions that must be challenged. Such statements give the impression that we have no choice over what we do or where we put our energy. Well, I have news for you. You are not a beggar and you have a choice! Don't let your postcode or your past rob you of the power of choice. It's yours. I'm not saying such choices are easy or without challenge – this will rarely if ever be the case – but too many abdicate their responsibility by accepting their so-called lot and believing "that life" cannot change. I am not merely talking of getting a better job or earning more money, perfectly acceptable things to do, rather I'm talking about doing the things that bring you to life. Sometimes to live your dream may involve a pay-cut or a harder route in the short term, but the pay-out can be huge emotionally and physically, yielding a far greater return than earning lots of money for a purpose we were not created for.

When I left Bible College I could have taken jobs that paid double and more than the amount I earned at my first church, but truly money wasn't the issue – purpose was. Money and financial security are important, but so often these things eclipse purpose and many end up giving their lives to things they really don't believe in. Here's a little test. If you would do what you're doing now for nothing, then you believe in it and the chances are it's what you should be doing. If you wouldn't do it for nothing, then why are you doing it now?

Look at these words of Jesus:

> "... the world must learn that I love the Father and that I do exactly what my Father has commanded me ..."
>
> (John 14:31)

Note the link between love and purpose. Theoretically, Jesus could have done His own thing, but He chose to do what the Father wanted. Why? Because He loved the Father. The Gospels make it clear that Jesus only said what the Father said, only did what the Father commanded and only went where the Father directed. There was no misplaced energy in the life of Jesus because His purpose came out of His personhood and His intimate understanding of His Father.

Before we move on let me ask you these questions:

- Why are you doing what you are doing?
- Does it energise you or demotivate you?
- Would you do it for free?

The answers will speak for themselves! Take courage.

Missed opportunity

My wife Dawn is currently engaged in the job of her dreams. Even when she was in Bible College she talked with excitement about administration and serving the church. For some, having the words administration and excitement in the same sentence is almost as ridiculous as putting chocolate and non-fat together. The two just don't go. Yet, for Dawn it's a fit. She loves it. However, she hasn't always had the job of her dreams. In fact, for the first few years of our marriage she served in administration, but in a secular job. She was able to use and develop her skills in this context and in hindsight it turned out to be brilliant training for her, but deep down she wanted it to be for the church. Throughout this period she served voluntarily within the church. As she did this, a small part-time post became available. She served and out of this came a role that is more or less full-time. Dawn could have had the mentality of waiting for the ideal opportunity to present itself. I suspect in that case she would still be waiting. Instead, she engaged her gift in the small and routine opportunities available. She lived out what she believed she was, even in a limited way, and as she did so, the opportunity she had been hoping for arose.

Undoubtedly, opportunities can be missed, probably because we're doing the wrong things, moving our lives in the wrong direction. Mistaken identity will inevitably lead to misplaced energy which will almost certainly ensure we miss great opportunities.

However, we can also miss opportunities because we refuse to engage in the less than ideal circumstances that present themselves to us. If it's not perfect, if the package isn't right, then we refuse to even consider it. I have found invariably that the willingness to serve leads to greater opportunities to do the things we know we've been called to. I love to see people engage even when I know it's not exactly what they wanted or hoped for and it's fun to see these ordinary opportunities develop into something much more significant.

On the cross, Jesus in defiant glory announced, *"It is finished"* (John 19:30). He had completed His work of saving the world and was now committing His spirit into the hands of His Father. However, I don't believe His finished work points only to the cross, but rather includes all that had gone before. Every footstep, touch, word, miracle, connection and action was all part of the work of Jesus. Jesus was not afraid to take His opportunities. Ralph Lewis did some research on the life of Jesus and he identified one hundred and twenty five encounters Jesus had with individuals recorded in the Gospels. He concluded that 54% of these episodes were initiated by the people in question and not by Jesus. In fact, he concluded that Jesus more often than not, responded to the opportunities presented to Him. It seems few opportunities escaped the Master.[11]

Jesus refused to be someone else and as a result He was Himself. There was never a case of mistaken identity as far as He was concerned. It seems out of this clear sense of personal identity He was able to channel His energy into the areas of most importance and effectiveness, and from this preoccupation with what was supremely important He did not miss an opportunity to touch His world and fulfil His destiny. Some thought he was the son of Joseph, but He knew He was the Son of God!

"Ah, that's Jesus," you say. "I'm not like Jesus, I'm me!" My point exactly! I'm not asking you to copy Jesus, but I am asking you to learn from Him. He represents a better way for us all, one where identity is nurtured and valued and from which purpose is celebrated and enjoyed. Surely life is too short to be spent being someone else, squandering our energy and opportunities on insignificant things. Learn to be yourself, love yourself and liberate yourself to touch the world as God designed and intended you to.

Notes

1. Emphasis added.
2. It was the same in His day. See John 1:10, 14.
3. Mark 6:1–6.
4. Luke 2:49–50.
5. Luke 4:18–19.
6. All found in John's gospel: I am the Bread of Life (6:35), I am the light of the world (8:12), I am the gate (10:7), I am the good shepherd (10:11), I am the resurrection (11:25), I am the way/truth/life (14:6) & I am the true vine (15:1).
7. John 4:34.
8. Luke 2:52.
9. Hebrews 5:8.
10. John 18:4–8.
11. Sweet, L., *The Gospel According to Starbucks*, Water Brook, 2007, p. 87.

The World Needs You

A man came home from work and found his children outside playing in the mud. They were still in their pyjamas and empty food boxes and wrappers were strewn across the front lawn. The door of his wife's car was open, as was the front door to the house and there was absolutely no sign of the dog. As he entered his home he found an even bigger mess. A lamp had been knocked over and his favourite rug was crumpled and squashed against the wall. In the lounge the Cartoon Channel was loudly blaring out to an empty room and toys as well as clothes were scattered across the floor.

As he moved to the kitchen, his jaw dropped as he saw the dishes piled high in the sink, the remains of breakfast left on the table, the fridge door wide open, dog food on the floor, a broken glass under the table and a small pile of sand spread across the back door. In panic he quickly ran up the stairs, stepping over toys and more clothes, as he was looking for his wife, now convinced that she was sick or incapacitated by injury. As he reached the landing, he was met by a small trickle of water as it made its way out of the bathroom door from a gently overflowing bath. Peering inside he observed the carnage of wet towels, scummy soap and sodden toys, not to mention toothpaste smeared on the mirror and miles of unravelled toilet paper.

As he rushed to the bedroom, he found his wife still curled up in bed in her pyjamas reading a novel. She looked up at him and smiled and asked him how his day had gone. He looked at her in bewilderment and asked, "What happened here today? Are you okay? Have you seen the mess in this house?" Without lifting her head from her novel, she smiled and answered, "You know how everyday when you come home from work you ask me what in the world I do all day?"

"Yes," he replied incredulously.

"Well, today I didn't do it!"

Think about this for just a moment or two. What would be the impact on *your* world if *you* decided not to turn up – if today and every day, you checked out of being the God-made person you are and decided to do something else or be someone else? When it comes to discovering our identity and living in the power of our destiny, the danger is that our focus becomes inward and our ambitions self-centred. However, what we need to realise, and I hope we've managed to do it before this chapter, is that everything we are and do impacts those around us and on the world we are called to touch. The discovery of the *self* we are in Christ is not merely to satisfy and placate our own needs, but to empower us to go to our world and pour out of ourselves into the emptiness of others what God has graciously and lavishly given to us.

When George Bailie stood on the snow covered bridge that Christmas Eve, he had convinced himself that everyone would be better off if he were dead. But that night, Clarence Odbody (an angel second class), showed George what his world would have looked like had he not been born, had he not been the man he was and not made the contribution he did. This rare gift allowed George to see just how important he was for himself and more significantly, how important he was for the many *others* in his life. As Clarence pointed out, "You see George, you really did have a wonderful life. Don't you see what a mistake it would be to throw it away?"[1]

In our pursuit of who we are, of discovering our true self in Christ, the danger is we make the journey all about us, when the truth is we're just one part of a gloriously big picture. Who I am and what I do (remember, identity is linked to destiny) is not just important for me, it's important for everyone around me – everyone who is touched by me.

This truth is perfectly illustrated by one of the greatest stories in the Old Testament. It centres on a young man called Joseph (Genesis 37:1–50:26). We first meet him as a precocious seventeen-year-old, the favourite son of his father, the recipient of a coloured coat and the object of sibling jealousy and hatred! This turbulent mix of dysfunctionality is further stirred by the announcement from young Joseph that he has had a dream. In his dream his sheaf of corn rose and stood upright, while the sheaves of his brothers gathered round and bowed down. The reaction of his brothers is understandably aggressive and the hatred against Joseph rises to critical levels. Now, at this stage one might think that the coloured-coat wearing one would keep his head down and let the dust settle. Oh no, not Joseph. He has another dream and this time he announces that the sun, moon and eleven stars bowed down to him. At this even his father rebuked him. (Joseph later wrote a book called *How to Win Friends and Influence People*, but for some reason he couldn't get it published.)

Joseph was undoubtedly a gifted individual with potential to make a gigantic impact on his world. The dreams God gave him were a hint of what the future held and that he would rise to be a leader par-excellence. However, as a seventeen-year-old all Joseph saw was everyone bowing to him. I suspect that Joseph interpreted the meaning of these two dreams as being about *him*! Over the next thirteen years of his journey he was to discover that those amazing dreams weren't so much about him, but about *them*! Through the anonymity of Potiphar's house and the obscurity of the king's prison he learned the life-changing lesson that the world did not revolve around him, but that he nonetheless had a crucial role to play and that if he played it well and continued to be his God-made self, doing what he was designed and created to do, then through enriching other people's worlds he would get to live and experience the fulfilment of his own dreams. Joseph served Potiphar's household so well that God's blessing was evident and the young Hebrew got a promotion.[2] The dreamer served the prison warden so well (Joseph had been put in prison on a false charge of attempted rape) that God's blessing was evident and yes, he got another promotion.[3] Joseph served the butler so well that eventually (after two years of waiting) the butler spoke up and got him out of prison.[4] Joseph served Pharaoh so well, arguably the most powerful man in the world at that time, that he made Joseph, a thirty-year-old Hebrew slave with a criminal record, the second most powerful man in the world.[5] Though Joseph discovered and remained true to who he was, his path to destiny was made possible primarily because of the grace of God, but also crucially because Joseph realised his dreams weren't about *him*, but about *them*!

Twenty-two years after his brothers unceremoniously dumped him down a pit they stood trembling before an Egyptian who had their destiny in his hands. In one of the most tender and moving parts of the story, Joseph, unable to contain his emotions, finally reveals himself to his brothers.

"I am Joseph! Is my father still living?"

(Genesis 45:3).

Up to that point he had spoken through an interpreter, but now he speaks in Hebrew. Until then they had known him as Zaphenath-Paneah, but now they discover his name is really Joseph. Though this moment was terrifying for the brothers it was the ultimate test of whether Joseph believed his dreams were about him or them. Read his words slowly:

> *"But God sent me ahead of you to preserve for you a remnant on earth and to save your lives by a great deliverance."*

(45:7)

Note will you, this verse has one reference to Joseph and three references to them. Father to Pharaoh and ruler of all Egypt he might have been, but at that moment Joseph knew why he was the way he was, why he had been given what he had and for whom all of this was intended. Though for sure he stood upright and they bowed down, Joseph, the now favoured son of Pharaoh, recipient of his signet ring and man of immense status and privilege, understood it wasn't about *him*, but about *them*!

What does Joseph teach us about the type of you the world needs?

The world needs *you* to be you

As part of the research for this book I tried to find out how many people called John Andrews lived in the United Kingdom. I was truly amazed by the findings. In the 2001 UK population census there were 325 people registered with *my* name. However, when the search was widened to include middle names (of which I have none) the number jumped to 1,113. Wow! All those people with my name and I've never met any of them! I decided to take my research a little further and Googled my name on the picture search. Loads of John Andrews wannabes showed up, *pretending to be me*! My wife assured me I was the best looking John Andrews on Google! I wonder how many people there are called John Andrews in the whole world? Answers on a post card to . . .

What's even more amazing than discovering that there are over one thousand John Andrews in the UK is the fact that no-matter who they are, none of them are me! They may be more talented, earn more money and delight in lots of facial hair, but that's as far as it goes. Yes, we share the commonality of a name and the fact that we are members of the human race, but I am the only John Andrews like me in the history of the world and God wants me as John Andrews to be me.

I've watched the movie *Spartacus* many times, but one scene gets me every time. The Romans have ruthlessly put down the rebellion inspired by Spartacus and now they are exacting their dreadful revenge. Looking over the bedraggled remains of the defeated army the Romans ask for Spartacus to identify himself. After a few minutes of hesitation, Spartacus (starring Kirk Douglas) is about to stand up, when another man beside him jumps to his feet and cries, "I'm Spartacus." Then another does the same and another . . . and so it continues until every man, in an attempt to protect their beloved leader, is screaming out, "I'm Spartacus!" Unfortunately, the Romans decide to kill them all!

When Joseph met his brothers after twenty-two years he was able to speak to them in his native tongue, not through an interpreter and declare, *"I am Joseph!"* (Genesis 45:3). He knew who he was and even though he looked, sounded and spoke like an Egyptian, the real Joseph was there all along doing what only Joseph could do.

The world needs the real you to stand up. It doesn't need you pretending to be someone else, or someone else having to try and be you because you haven't shown up. Your world needs you to be able to stand up and say, "I'm Spar..." No, don't say "Spartacus", that won't work, especially if your name is Rachel; but stand up and proclaim who you are. As the Bard put it:

> "This above all – to thine own self be true,
> and it must follow, as the night the day,
> Thou canst not then be false to any man." [6]

Believe it or not, there is no one like you and in fact no other human being can do what only you can do. Oh yes, others can do the same thing as you, but none of them can do it like you, because you are the only you there is!

The world needs *you* to turn up

It happens every time at every award ceremony I've ever seen. "And the winner is . . ." The music erupts, the crowd goes wild and the presenters look a little uneasy because they know what's coming next. "We're sorry the winner can't be with us today as they are at home washing their hair, but they sent along their gardener to receive the award." What a disappointment. The audience, many of whom paid a fortune for the privilege of being there, were hoping to see their favourite TV, music or movie star and instead, they got the gardener!

I don't know if you've ever been disappointed by a no-show, but of all the things in life that wind me up, this is in the top three. "Sorry I didn't make it pastor, but I was with you in spirit." Yeah right. Well it wasn't your spirit I needed – I needed your energy, talents, input and creativity all wrapped up in your body! Most of us take the no-show (and I'm not just talking about appointments) too lightly. When we don't show, when someone doesn't turn up and contribute who they are into that moment, then everyone is poorer and we all lose out. Life goes on, people manage, I understand all of that, but think how much better life would have been and how much better they would have managed had you turned up. Many, like the wife at the beginning of this chapter (no, it wasn't Dawn), are never truly missed until for some reason they don't show. Suddenly, there's a gap and we realise the powerful contribution that one person's presence and life can make.

What's remarkable about Joseph is that he just kept turning up, whether it is in Potiphar's house, the prison or to Pharaoh. Some would like to argue he didn't have a choice in each of these examples. That's true, but of course we all know that it's possible to turn up and not give of oneself in a positive way! It was because Joseph turned up every day that the people around him were blessed and the nations of Egypt and Israel (and arguably many other nations) were saved. Can you imagine the impact had he not turned up?

Your world needs you to show up. When you, the only you in the universe, don't turn up, your world is poorer because of it. They need you to be there – and you need you to be there.

The world needs *you* to contribute

Have you ever heard the expression "the lights are on but nobody's home"? It points to the concept of being present but somehow, at the same time, being somewhere else. Our body is in the building but our mind is enjoying a large latte at Starbucks. In such a scenario the person might as well not be there.

Joseph was a contributor. His ability to contribute in the variety of the circumstances he found himself in, none of which he was trained for, not only created opportunities for him, but improved and enriched the lives (with the exception of the baker) of everyone he encountered. His determination to continue to give when everyone would have understood his reluctance is remarkable. He serves Potiphar, the prison warden, Pharaoh and even the butler "as unto the Lord" and it's this quality of contribution which both gets him noticed and benefits the recipients.

There is no point showing up and not giving of ourselves. "Well, I'm here aren't I?" Yes, but why? What's the point in being here if all you are going to do is suck the oxygen out of the building? What are you going to give, what impact are you going to make, what unique contribution are you going to place on the table so that the world you inhabit becomes a better place, not just for you, but for everyone? In giving, Joseph got back much more than he ever bargained for and so will we. If we are prepared to not only turn up, but also give out, we will be better people and our world will celebrate our lives.

I suppose one of the dangers of the message of this book is that it can become lost in translation when filtered through the self-obsessed value system of a modern generation dominated by, as one man put it, the world of the *hyphenated self*. Christian thought has always been uncomfortable with talk of self-elevation or self-promotion and the language contained in the pages of this book thus far may cause some to suggest my motivation is rooted more in the world of positive psychology than biblical theology. Our comfort zone in this area is often encapsulated by the words of John the Baptist when he cried, *"He must become greater; I must become less"* (John 3:30). The call to self-denial seems to sit uncomfortably with talk of self-discovery and the pursuit of our identity.

However, what must be understood is that the goal of discovering our true identity, our God-made self, is not to further indulge our obsession with self, but rather to empower us to be what we were divinely intended to be and thus fulfil the mandate of heaven over our lives. True Christianity has at its core not the individual but the glory and majesty of the One true and living God, who through Jesus, His Son in flesh, saved the world. However, the message of true Christianity is one of God's love to humankind in an attempt to reach them, liberate them and elevate them. This glorious celebration of the individual and God's personal obsession with those individuals can make it seem like all this, the world and everything in it, is about "me". But, in the same way that the earth is not the centre of the universe, you and I are not the centre of the world. The worst form of idolatry is to make God in our own image, attempting to make Him fit into our small thinking and the limitation of our world. Discovering who we truly are has the potential to lift our vision off the world of the hyphenated self and into the world of our glorious God. Being able to say, "I am Joseph!" is not a sin. However, making this revelation the central hub of our world most certainly is.

Discovering who you are is not just about you, it's about them! Living a fulfilled and happy life must never become a singular obsession of individualistic thinking, rather it should be the by-product of revealed truth in us and the means to be a blessing to others. Life as a whole-self must not be, in fact cannot be, limited to personal gratification, but used for the pursuit of wholeness in others. The world needs you! It does not need you preoccupied with self-gain, -pain or -fame; rather it needs people who know who they are and why they are here. Our world needs people who, like Joseph, have discovered the life-changing truth: "It's not all about me . . . *it's also about them!*"

Notes _____

1. From the movie, *It's a Wonderful Life*, The Collector's Edition . . . and my favourite movie of all time.
2. Genesis 39:1–6.
3. Genesis 39:20–23.
4. Genesis 40:1–41:13.
5. Genesis 41:14–45.
6. Shakespeare, W., *The Tragedy of Hamlet, Prince of Denmark*, Act I, scene iii, Polonius speaking.

Nobility Obliges

"Harry the Nazi!" That was one of the newspaper headlines that greeted Prince Harry, third in line to the British monarchy, after attending a friend's fancy dress party themed, "Colonial and Native" in January 2005. Unfortunately, the young Prince dressed in a World War II German army desert uniform and sported a Nazi armband. Though he apologized immediately, it was a tremendous embarrassment to the Royal Family, provoking criticism from numerous quarters across the United Kingdom and the world. For many, the struggle against Nazi Germany was not merely a note in history but something deeply personal and costly. Few would ever have believed it possible that a Royal son, for whatever reason, would identify himself with such a hideous symbol and the philosophy it represented. His indiscretion was even more poignant as it occurred only a couple of weeks before 27th January, earmarked as Holocaust Memorial Day, commemorating the death of millions in Nazi death camps.

The ultimate proof of who we believe we are is demonstrated in how we live. If we believe we are sons of the King of kings and Lord of lords, then our lifestyles will be a reflection of such a conviction, demonstrated in a life lived nobly, honouring both God and ourselves. If we believe our lives are God-made and purpose-filled, then we will take our most precious commodity seriously, taking care to nurture what we have and giving a good account of our personhood and gifts. If, on the other hand, we believe that our lives are more about genetics than genius, of little value and insignificant in the grand scheme of things, then the tendency will be to squander the best of who we are on that which is least important. Whatever we think about ourselves, that conclusion will determine not only how we live, but what live for.

The ambition of this book has been to deny the enemy of our souls the opportunity to steal from us something that is rightfully ours. John's Gospel declares that for those who believe, God gives the right to be called children of God. The devil is terrified by the prospect that any person could discover who they really are, understand their position in Christ and live their lives accordingly. Such a person, such a life, is truly representative of God's Kingdom on the earth and a devastating weapon against the kingdom of darkness. That's why using whatever means are at his disposal, he will do everything he can to steal, corrupt or kill the truth of our God-made self, thus not only eradicating our identity, but destroying our destiny. He knows that if we know we are sons of God, nobility will pulsate in us and flow through us to a world hungry to know the truth of who they are.

A four-year-old was at the clinic for a check up. As the doctor looked into her ears he asked, "Do you think I'll find Peter Rabbit in here?" The little girl said nothing. Next the doctor looked down her throat. He asked, "Do you think I'll see The Munch Bunch down there?" Again, the little girl was silent. Then the doctor put a stethoscope to her chest. As he listened to her heartbeat, he asked, "Do you think I'll hear Barbie in there?" "Oh, no," the little girl replied. "Jesus is in my heart. Barbie is on my socks!"

Knowing that we are in Jesus and He is in us will make all the difference as to how we face our world and its probing questions. The glorious truth is that you are in Christ and He is in you. The challenge that now faces us is living out who we believe we are, demonstrating to the world around us what a son of the King looks like. Paul puts it this way:

> *"As a prisoner for the Lord, then, I urge you to live a life worthy of the calling you have received."*
>
> (Ephesians 4:1)

Paul begs us to live a worthy life. We'll get to what "worthy" means in a moment, but notice the basis on which he makes this passionate request. The first basis of his appeal is on that which has gone before. This statement follows three chapters of glorious theological insights into who we are in Christ. Of the fourteen references to being in Christ contained in the book of Ephesians, thirteen of them occur in the first three chapters. From the outset his language is victorious and assured, setting the tone for the whole letter:

> *"Praise be to the God and Father of our Lord Jesus Christ, who has blessed us in heavenly realms with every spiritual blessing **in Christ**."*
>
> (Ephesians 1:3, emphasis added)

The second basis of his appeal is the calling of God: "... *of the calling you have received.*" The word Paul uses here points to the idea of divine summons. This is not a casual, "I'll do it if I feel like it", this is a life lived in response to a clear understanding of the call that has been issued by God Himself. This summons is both serious and uncompromising. God isn't messing and neither should we be. Through His lavish grace He has issued an invitation to walk with Him. Our understanding of this call will impact the way in which we live.

Paul wants us to *"live a life worthy"*. The word "worthy", used as an adverb as in this context, suggests living our lives in a manner worthy of a lifestyle befitting or becoming our status; living right on the basis of fitness. The adjective points to "having the weight of" (weighing as much as) another thing. It means that our lives should "weigh" as much as that which we seek to follow. Our lives should be of equal measure to the claim that we are in Christ, that in fact we are following a divine summons, that we are what we claim to be, that we preach what we practise! Paul likes this word and often uses it in the context of our calling and relationship with God in Christ. In his mind there can be no divorcing how we live according to who we believe we are, and to whom we belong.[1]

So, how can we live as sons of our Father, demonstrating the nobility of our status?

Like Father like son

> *"How great is the love the Father has lavished on us, that we should be called children of God! And that is what we are!"*

(1 John 3:1)

The great temptation is to reduce our heavenly Father to our image than for us to conform to His. One of the dangers of shrinking Him to our dimensions is that self-image will be distorted. If God is just like us, our mate, then it becomes much easier to justify any behaviour which we deem is acceptable to Him, without consulting Him. If, however, we rise to the challenge of the divine summons and provoke ourselves to reflect Him, rather than trying to get Him to reflect us, then transformational change will be part and parcel of our journey.

When challenged to *"live a life worthy..."* too many today talk in terms of what they feel or what they think God might like them to do, without allowing their minds to be elevated to His level by considering His truth, thus confronting their thinking at their level. You and I may feel a lot of things and allow ourselves the liberty to assume what God might think, but at some point, if we're serious about the divine summons we've received, if we believe that the Father has lavished His love on us and made us sons, then we need to take seriously what He says and what He wants.

Over the years I've had to endure the most demeaning excuses of sons as they've tried to justify their less than worthy behaviour. Believe me, I've heard it all. I never realised God was so chilled when it came to pride, unforgiveness, greed, drunkenness, adultery, drug taking and even drug selling. As these *sons* have tried to convince me (perhaps really trying to convince themselves) that their actions can somehow squeeze into the word "worthy", I've marvelled at their meagre and impoverished view of a Father that would endorse such behaviour as a reflection of Himself. Is this what it means to live in Christ, to respond to the divine summons, to show what the Father looks like through the lens of our definition of sonship?

Would our Father be "embarrassed" by the antics of His children? Would He have to issue an apology for our actions because they have offended not only Him, but the world He's trying to save?

If we claim to be sons of a King, then surely we should live like one. We must be careful that we are not living as sons of a "me-sized Father", but rather we are seeking to live our lives to "Father-sized" proportions. The former is idolatry, while the latter is liberty!

Love your neighbour as *yourself*

> "... Every day I fight a war against the mirror,
>   I can't take the person starin' back at me.
> I'm a hazard to myself, don't let me get me,
> I'm my own worst enemy,
>   it's bad when you annoy yourself,

So irritating, don't want to be my friend no more,
I want to be somebody else...
So doctor, doctor won't you please prescribe me something,
    a day in the life of someone else...''[2]

If we don't love ourselves we're going to find it hard to respect
ourselves and live noble lives. It's impossible to live as a son when
we are certain we are slaves. If we struggle to love who we are,
we're going to find it challenging to love those around us.

When asked His view of what was the greatest commandment,
Jesus gave a staggering answer. In one sense Jesus was onto a loser;
no matter how He answered, He was going to be wrong.
However, his response confounded everyone listening:

> '' 'Love the Lord your God with all your heart and with all your soul and
> with all your mind.' This is the first and greatest commandment. And
> the second is like it: 'Love your neighbour as yourself.' ''
>
> (Matthew 22:37–39)

It is interesting that the same word used to express our love for God
is used when referring to our neighbour and, it could be argued,
implies to ourselves. Jesus told us to love those around us as
ourselves. Does part of the greatest commandments given to us by
Jesus endorse "self-love"? Yes, it does, but not in the self-absorbed,
ego-centric way most will choose to understand this. When we
understand the context of this self-love we observe that it is not
merely about us and our personal gratification. We cannot focus on
self-love in a biblical context unless we are prepared to talk about
God-love and neighbour-love! Only then can we truly enjoy God-
intended self-love. We must not be confused at such terms.
Self-love as found in the Bible is a love which more properly allows
us to engage with others. Through this it is God's intention that a
whole and happy self is able to make a powerful contribution to our

surrounding environment, thus enriching others out of the wealth of a secure self-image.

It is not God's plan that we should war against the person we see in the mirror or that our self-loathing is such that we long to be somebody else, even if its only for a day. This does not negate the fact that we have to address issues of self-development or growth, or that we have to contend with aspects of our personhood and character which are out of sync with God. However, if we are to make the journey of change then we must begin from the right place, a place where we know we are loved by God and where the person we are is fundamentally valued and important. Part of living a life worthy of our calling is accepting who we are. Not loving ourselves reflects badly on the Father who made us and on the validity of the life-changing faith we claim to possess. The desire to be better and to improve must always be held in balance with the fact that right now we are already children of God. Like most parents, I want my children to be the best they can be, to achieve in school and dare courageously in life, but I want them to go into their world filled with the knowledge that they are special to me and loved by me, thus empowering them to see themselves through heaven's eyes, accepting themselves for who they truly are.

Live in the moment

" . . . making the most of every opportunity . . . "

(Ephesians 5:16)

If you've got a clock or a watch that counts off seconds, stop reading this book now and look at it for ten seconds. Doesn't time fly when you are enjoying yourself? You've just witnessed the passing of ten seconds that will never come again. Oh, many more seconds lie ahead of you, I hope, but the ten that have gone are never coming back. One of the ways we live worthy is by living in the moment God has given us, by being the people God intended us to be. *The Message* puts it this way: *"Don't live carelessly, unthinkingly..."*

Knowing who we are helps us to take the moment and live it well, as Manning puts it *"...being fully present in the now is perhaps the premier skill of the spiritual life";*[3] giving ourselves to the "now here" (nowhere) in such a way that the moment is fully enjoyed and nothing is missed. When I read this verse as a child the phrase that I remembered was "redeem the time". That's the imagery behind Paul's words here. The word means "to buy up", "to ransom" or "rescue from loss". In other words, we are to do everything in our power to ensure no opportunity afforded to us is lost. Though we're trading in moments, the currency used to buy such a commodity is our words, actions and lifestyle. From the revelation of who we are flows a belief system which empowers a lifestyle that ensures we don't miss a thing. If, however, we're trying to be somebody else or "warring" with ourselves, our focus will not be on the opportunities all around us and the chances are we'll miss what is right in front of us.

When King Saul needed relief from an evil spirit that was tormenting him it was decided to find someone who could play the harp, the train of thought being, when they played the harp the evil spirit would leave. As the word got out, one of Saul's servants spoke up:

> *"I have seen a son of Jesse in Bethlehem who knows how to play the harp. He is a brave man and a warrior. He speaks well and is a fine-looking man. And the Lord is with him."*

> (1 Samuel 16:18)

David was invited into the presence of the king and ultimately the service of the king because he was good at playing the harp. His love of music and singing, evident to us in his many psalms, was no doubt developed out on the hills as he looked after his father's sheep. Little did he know that teaching himself how to play the harp would create an opportunity for him to serve his king and country. The thing is, previous to this invitation David had been anointed as the next king of Israel, ironically to succeed the man he was now being asked to serve.[4] When Samuel left, David could have easily resigned from his shepherd position and set up his own "David soon-to-be-king ministries". However, what seems to have happened is that David went back to his sheep, picked up his harp again and kept doing what he knew he should do. He lived in the moment. Amazingly, as he bought those moments on the hillside, ensuring no opportunity was lost, that pushed open the door through which David would enter royal service.

Too many are waiting for the moment instead of living in the moment. While we're waiting for something to happen we can miss what we could have done, thus scorning an opportunity that just might be the thing that takes us to a new adventure ... you know, the one we've been waiting for! As a friend of mine once said, "Big doors swing on small hinges." The ability to play the harp was such a small hinge, but the door it opened was huge! David screams at us, don't miss the moments, no-matter how ordinary they seem, because in the ordinary there is opportunity. "Whether you are hiking the Himalayas or hanging on to a subway strap in Staten Island, dunking a doughnut in Denver or sipping a Slurry in Sausalito, the geography of Nowhere (now here) encompasses Every/where."[5] Wherever you are now, live in the moment.

It's time to celebrate

A man and his wife both reached the age of fifty. The man prayed, "Lord, could you make my wife thirty years younger than me, please?" The Lord replied, "Are you sure you want me to do that?" "Yes, yes," said the man, "I'd really love it." "Okay," said God and the man suddenly found himself eighty years old. It's all too easy to wish our lives away, either because we don't like the one we've got, or we haven't quite attained the one we'd really like. Thirty years of our lives can be wasted wishing on a star, hoping for a change, lamenting our loss and complaining at our lot. "If only" becomes our mantra, but the only reward it brings us is frustration and disappointment.

After his brothers had sold Joseph as a slave, they returned to their father Jacob to break the bad news, only their version of events had changed slightly between Dothan and home. The news flash mentioned wild animals and torn flesh, but nothing about pits and treachery. When the brothers presented Joseph's torn and bloodied cloak to Jacob, his father's response was predictable:

> " 'It is my son's robe! Some ferocious animal has devoured him. Joseph has surely been torn to pieces,' and Jacob refused to be comforted."
>
> (Genesis 37:33–35)

The awful tragedy of this episode is that Jacob lived the next twenty-two years of his life under the cloud of a lie and as a result precious time was stolen from him, time spent in mourning, not celebration. That's the terrible power of a lie. When we believe it, it becomes the truth (at least to us) and we end up living according to its dictates. Like Jacob, it is all too easy to believe a lie and end up living by it as if it was truth.

It's time to break through the prison walls of the lies you have been fed and dare to believe the truth of what God says about you. The lies that may have come from your past, your peers or even your parents can only hold you as long as you believe them. Once you learn the truth, the power of the lie is broken and you are free. That's what happened to Jacob. When the brothers returned from Egypt, having encountered Joseph, they told their father everything. Though at first Jacob refused to believe it, he eventually became convinced, and the Bible says, *"... the spirit of their father revived"*, and he promptly made the journey to see his son.[6] That's the power of truth, in an instant it not only broke through the prison walls of the lies Jacob had believed, but it infused the old patriarch with enough energy to get up from his mourning and make a journey of destiny.

Whose report are you going to believe? Are you going to believe the words of people or the words of God? Are you going to allow the lies to doom you to a life of mourning, repeating your "if only" and blaming God for not making you somebody else? If you chose to live like this, you'll blink your eyes and half your life will have gone. Ten more years will have made you no wiser and the weeds of regret will have grown up around your feet. But it doesn't have to be like that. Today, right here, right now you have a choice. You can complain or celebrate. You can lament the person you're not and the things you haven't done, or you can start to celebrate the person you are and begin to make a contribution that only you can, thus enriching yourself and your world. What's it to be?

The nobility of our birth demands we live life well. The realisation that we are children of God, divinely summonsed by the voice of God Himself must surely elevate our sense of value and worth and provoke us. To know that our names are written on the palm of His hand and that we are fearfully and wonderfully made for an eternal purpose, should fill us with hope. To know that heaven looks at us and sees the person we were meant to be, the potential within us and the purpose for which we were created should energise us to live in the moment and celebrate the day. God knows who you are and has moved heaven and hell to convince you of this truth. The devil knows who you are and is using all his wicked wiles to keep you from discovering the truth. However, the biggest question in all is this ... do you know who you are?

"Fear not, for I have redeemed you;
I have summoned you by name;
you are mine."
(Isaiah 43:1)

Notes

1. See also Philippians 1:27, Colossians 1:10, 1 Thessalonians 2:12 & 2 Thessalonians 1:11 where he uses the same word.
2. Pink, *Don't Let Me Get Me*, from Album M!ssundaztood, Arista Records 2001.
3. Manning, *Ruthless Trust*, p. 150. He makes a play on the word "nowhere" to mean "now here".
4. 1 Samuel 16:1–13.
5. Manning, *Ruthless Trust*, p. 161.
6. Genesis 45:25–28.

We hope you enjoyed reading this New Wine book.
For details of other New Wine books
and a range of 2,000 titles from other
Word and Spirit publishers visit our website:
www.newwineministries.co.uk
email: newwine@xalt.co.uk